Ultimate Betrayal:

The Sex Abuse Case against Dr. Earl Bradley

Ultimate Betrayal:

The Sex Abuse Case against Dr. Earl Bradley

A True Story
by Meg Ellacott
Rehoboth Beach, Delaware

Most names in this book have been changed to protect the innocent. Some real locations are mentioned for historic and background reasons but the names connected to those locations have been made up.

Copyright ©2013 by Meg Ellacott
ISBN-13: 978-1482335927
ISBN-10: 1482335921

Additional copies can be purchased via:
CreateSpace.com/4131027
Amazon.com
Select stores in Delaware

Dedicated to the professionals and caregivers who protect our children.

To the brave parents, family members and our medical community who survived him.

Acknowledgements

When I decided to write this book, I had no idea it would become real. A non-fiction, true-crime, written from first-person point-of-view, kind of book.

One I never really thought I'd finish.

One I never thought I was capable of creating.

It was far more difficult than I imagined. At times writing it was tremendously painful. Other times, it was rewarding because I knew I was chronicling an important story. One that should never just *go away*.

Now it is time to thank friends, classmates and writers, especially those with the Rehoboth Beach Writers' Guild, who stood beside me and believed in me while I wrote this book.

I am so very grateful to them.

One in particular is Maribeth Fischer, a truly gifted writer, a published author of *The Life You Longed For*, (2007, Simon and Schuster) a talented teacher and editor who spent many patient hours with me on the manuscript and encouraged me every step of the way. She became my mentor, my mantra "what would Maribeth do?" and my friend. Without her, this book would not have happened. Thank you for all you did, Maribeth, and know that the Rehoboth Beach Writers' Guild, your creation, your gift, means everything to me.

To Steve Robison, my multi-talented publisher, photographer, friend and poetry writer who is also our local wizard in social networking and website design, who made my book come alive. Thanks to Steve and Red Sky Websites.

To Amy, Becky and Deb – my family and closest friends – thank you for your support.

To Daria, also a good friend and a superb author herself who wrote the book, *Untying the Knot;*, please know how important your insight, comments and encouragement were to me.

To my fellow writer friends in the classes, free-writes and readings: To those of you who gave me gentle yet honest feedback – I am eternally grateful for your ideas and thoughts. Your questions led me to dig, and to write deeper. They were encouraging, constructive and insightful – and I thank you for your fortitude and sitting through my, sometimes difficult to hear, readings.

I also wish to thank Hazel Brittingham, our resident historian, for her wonderful book: *Lantern on Lewes*.

To the *News Journal* and *Cape Gazette* journalists, I am grateful and thank you for your clear and concise reporting on this difficult topic.

To the families, friends and patients who survived him, thank you for your trust and for sharing your stories with me.

Foreword

I could begin with my struggle to write all these pages about a pedophile pediatrician but I won't. This will come later in the book after I have found my voice, after I have learned where this story leads me. For now I will start with what fascinated me and what appalled me at the same time. Like a freight train about to run off its tracks or an impending car crash, the story of this diabolical doctor would grab my attention within days of his arrest and never let me go until years later. Only after I'd had my fill,
    only after I learned about criminal minds and about the abuse of children,
        only after I'd felt compelled to write all these pages,
        only after learning more than I wanted to about secrets in a small town –
        only then would I begin to let go.

Part I: Winter 2010

"Evil is always unspectacular and always human. It shares our bed and eats at our table."
anonymous

Pediatrician

The medical practice of Dr. Earl Brian Bradley is closed since his arrest a month ago in December 2009.

The play-land-type practice sits idle now. The name of the practice, Baybees, was another silly little game of Bradley's. Situated by the bay and obsessed with bumblebees, Bradley named his medical practice Baybees, a play on the word, *babies*.

Like the ones he raped.

Deserted and appearing almost haunted, the grounds and the buildings remain under a spell of eerie silence. Early January and the cold wind of winter whistles through the dilapidated 'baby' Ferris wheel that sits in front of the main building of the practice. That same wind whines through the cut holes of the bronze statue of children playing a pretend game of ring around the rosie perched on the roof of the building. Just behind the statue stands the giant blue sign atop the building, as big as the building itself, with red lettering that says Baybees Pediatrics, *www.baybees.org*.

It is just weeks since the arrest and I have a strong urge to go to the property. I sit in my car viewing the place where most of Earl Bradley's crimes took place. I cannot bring myself to go 'on property' so I stay in my car on the little side street. It is silent except for the whir of the car heater. The make-believe school bell sits next to the play fortress big enough for one child. And his silly little, bright yellow Volkswagen Beetle car is ever present, ever rusting.

It's below freezing but the sun will soon warm the air. It glints off the speeding cars that charge by Bradley's practice. No one looks; no one wants to acknowledge the building; a reminder of Bradley's evil actions that now consume our community. It's as if the building were invisible, despite the Christmas lights strung along the roof that glitter in the waning sunlight.

Debris blows through the parking lot and it is everywhere. Winter winds trash the business that once flourished. Sadness, chaos and bitterness abound. Toys and Big Wheels litter the driveway and the parking lot. The lighted LED sign on the west side of the building is bashed in, maybe by a parent whose child was one of Bradley's victims; one wielding a baseball bat toward the sign as if it were Bradley's head.

Next door to Baybees sits the Lazy Susan Restaurant. *"Big Fat Crabs"* its sign reads. *Thanks for a great season. Cya next Spring!"* The Mountain Dew soda machine next to the entrance to the practice lays on its side now. Everything is weather-worn, beaten-down, like almost anyone who came in contact with Dr. Bradley.

Pedophile

No one knowingly hides a pedophile. But then, how did he get away with it for so long? How could it have taken fourteen years to stop him? How could the system have failed so many, so miserably?

The medical practice Bradley once dreamed of would become a place where people felt like part of a family. He imagined himself a "Norman Rockwell" type country doctor. In 2001 he bought the land and created his 'fun house' pediatrician practice on prime real estate just off Coastal Highway, Route 1 in Lewes, Delaware. His office featured a theater where cartoons were shown and a Disney-themed examination room. He distributed bumblebee snugglers to his tiny patients and had one room dedicated to the painter Norman Rockwell.

During a time when a nation saw a very different picture of war and discord, Rockwell chose to fill his paintings with the small details and nuances of everyday life: Mom in her starched apron serving Thanksgiving turkey; a country doctor in his stark white medical coat about to administer a vaccine. The idealistic, ordinary people in his paintings evoke a longing for a time and place that existed only in Rockwell's rich imagination, a more innocent time. For in Rockwell's personal life he harbored deep insecurities about his work, his ability to connect and the type of life he chose to live. While he tapped into a kinder and gentler time in his paintings, his own life was one of sadness, depression and loss. One psychiatric doctor told Rockwell, "You paint happiness, but do not live it."

Had Bradley connected with the artist because he too never fit in? His own insecurities never allowing him to?

Another exam room had a Pinocchio theme. Pinocchio, the liar, the boy puppet ill-treated by his father. Bradley once said he wanted to have people wonder what crazy Dr. Bradley would do next. "I want kids, as they grow up, to have all different memories of coming here."

His patients *would* have different memories; some, perhaps many, would not be the kind Rockwell depicted.

I turn up the heat in the car now and think of Bradley's arrest only a few weeks ago. Next to me sits one of several articles from the *Cape Gazette* Newspaper. "On December 18 2009, the Lewes pediatrician, 56, was arrested by Delaware State Police on three charges relating to an alleged rape of a 3 year-old female patient. The arresting officer said the charges were the result of a yearlong investigation." The 3-year-old, referred to as Jane Doe #1, I will call 'Melissa.' Police had received a warrant to search Bradley's Lewes office and detectives removed several computers, surveillance cameras and medical files. On that day, Bradley was charged with second-degree rape, first degree unlawful sexual contact and first degree endangering the welfare of a child. All three charges were felonies.

No one knew then that this would be only the beginning of what would become a full blown, unprecedented tragedy that would rock the small Delaware beach towns of Lewes and Rehoboth; one that could ultimately involve up to 100 victims. Bradley's crimes soon came to be known as *the* worst case of <u>documented</u> child molestation in the country, ever.

Faith

Long before Earl Bradley was convicted in December 2009, the evidence, rumors and secrets about a pediatrician who'd shown signs of abusing children amplified. Bradley became an artist at luring children and distracting their parents. People often doubt their instincts. They often second guess themselves. Fear starts deep down in the gut and begins to grow but is often ignored, pushed aside because 'it' just couldn't happen. That fear often begins with the slightest twinge that something taken for granted can no longer be trusted. A slice of a shadow darkens a place that only a moment before was sunny, and a cold draft destroys that warmth. For the mother of Jane Doe #1 – Melissa – what was solid suddenly became fragile on a chilly November day in 2009.

Nowhere, perhaps, are the limits of modern medicine more important than in the care of children, in the field of pediatrics. For most parents, the relationship and care of their child runs *mostly* on faith:

Faith that the doctor can and will heal their child.

Faith that their doctor will do his utmost to give medical care.

When that faith fails, the results can be devastating.

In December of 2009 Bradley would finally be stopped. In this same month, it would become the case that would haunt our small town and serve as a warning sign to doctors and families everywhere.

Melissa

I imagine Melissa's mother's discomfort grew the longer she sat in the waiting room. Turning to another mother she might have asked how long she'd been coming to Dr. Bradley.

"For about a year," the other mother might have easily replied. "I like him, don't you?"

Did Melissa's mother's stomach lurch the longer she sat, the longer she waited?

Something wasn't right.

She had, in fact, always liked Dr. 'B' but at that moment she was beginning to wonder where they were. He'd asked her to wait 'just a minute' while he took Melissa to get her prize.

But they'd been gone for too long now.

Still sitting outside his once-thriving medical practice I imagine the growing fear Melissa's Mom must have experienced. How she might have felt that tingling in her hands, the pit in her stomach.

Was she worrying over nothing? Was she being silly? Perhaps she moved to the receptionist's window now and spoke more calmly than she felt. "Betsy, where's Melissa? Can you take me to them please?"

Perhaps she didn't wait for Betsy. Maybe she'd already begun moving toward the exam rooms.

Just as she turned the corner she might have heard Dr. Bradley bellow, "And here we are, Mom. I'm so proud of this young lady. What a good girl!" He asked her for another kiss, but she shook her head 'no' and moved quickly toward her mother.

This part I don't have to imagine – it was reported in the papers. When they reached the car, Melissa's mom asked what was wrong. He daughter seemed unusually quiet. Her daughter said that Bradley had hurt her while getting her toy. "He hurt my hiney, Mommy." This is just one of hundreds of reports still to come but *this* is how the case breaks open.

Again, I imagine this mother frantically pulled back in to the parking spot she'd just vacated and grabbed her cell to call her husband. "Answer the phone damn it, answer!" she almost screamed. Trying to stay calm she told him what their daughter had just said about the doctor visit.

"That's weird," he responded. "She said the same kind of thing back in October when we were at Baybees." I'd imagined this parking lot scene, but the part about the husband and wife coming to this same, alarming conclusion about Bradley was reported in the papers. Fear, confusion, rage – I cannot begin to imagine *what* those parents felt on that day in November 2009.

When the two parents realized the truth, they went to the police and this provided the final evidence to get the search warrant. *This* is what the attorney general's office had been waiting for – probable cause.

Thank God Melissa's family had come forward. It opened the door for all the other families. But,

The worst part was the not knowing.

The worst part was the fear.

The worst part was the sheer outrage they'd feel as the case unfolded. What had their children been made to endure? Parents did not know if their child was one of his victims; if their child was one that would be seen on the confiscated videos.

The computer files and surveillance cameras taken from Bradley's home and office would eventually show horrific scenes of child sexual abuse. One child had been so terrified, so badly tortured when Bradley forced her to orally copulate him, that she appeared to lose conscientiousness. This news had leaked out followed by a gag order. All I could think was My God, little girls, babies almost die less than 300 feet from where fathers and mothers calmly read newspapers or watched TV waiting for their daughters return. Bradley would revive them, dry their tears

sometimes with a teddy bear,

sometimes with a cold popsicle and bring them upstairs with a lollipop.

Sometimes in less than four minutes.

The Arrest

Bradley's arrest came nine days before Christmas 2009, and I, like so many, was feeling that annual holiday panic: Company coming, last minute Christmas presents, decorating the house. Already it was freezing cold, just six weeks before the blizzards of 2010 that would cripple most of Delaware.

I don't recall exactly where I was when I first heard the brief news blurb about the arrest. Most likely at home and it might have been WBOC's 6:00 local news. Daylight savings was long gone, so it would have been dark and chilly as I sat on my bed, remote in hand. I work from my home so at the end of the day, my habit is to walk the few steps from my office in the back of the house, a latte in hand, and flip on the news in the master bedroom. On that day, December 16, when Earl Bradley was first arrested and then released on $36,000 bail, I could not know how this would impact hundreds of lives, our local hospital, state laws and the very foundation of our town. Nor could I have fathomed how it would impact me.

Two days later, Bradley was arrested again after detectives began their review of the evidence.

Anguish

When I started writing these pages in January 2010, I thought it would be about a pedophile doctor named Earl Bradley.

I thought it would be about a heinous criminal case – never knowing it would turn into the largest documented child molestation case in history.

Do notice the word *documented*. There were fourteen hours of video tape of Bradley committing crimes against children.

I thought this story would be about a deranged predator.

I thought it would be about a parent's worst nightmare, one they could never bear to contemplate.

Instead I found it would not only be about him, but about me. About coming home.

About trust and about a small town torn apart.

About loss; and how easily confidence can come undone.

About life breaking into distracted fragments; about profound grief.

About lost innocence – long forgotten now.

The talk in town came in ripples. This criminal case, the state vs. Earl B. Bradley, was like a stone tossed into our Silver Lake, it's impact rippling out until all the waters are churned, until almost everyone felt its effects: families whose children had been violated, lawyers both criminal and civil, local police, the state justice system, the local hospital, family counseling centers, the townspeople and me.

How could I have known then how utterly unprepared I'd be for this to magnify to the extent it did?

How could I have been prepared for this to happen here at the beach?

Down the street from my new home?

Here, in this idyllic place – the one I'd searched for half my life.

How, in this small town known as the first town in the first state, could anyone have been prepared to learn that it was a pediatrician? A doctor who would be found guilty of raping over 100 children, some as young as three months old.

A doctor some so admired and once-beloved, a man known as Doctor 'B.'

A doctor devoted to a foundation that helped families who'd lost a child.

A doctor who met parents at the local hospital at two in the morning with a sick child.

A doctor who played Santa Claus in the local Christmas parade.

A doctor who left those who knew him reeling in disbelief.

"He fooled all of us" said a physician's assistant.

My Childhood

Why, though, did I begin writing this? Again and again, this is the question people ask. I am not a reporter, I have no children and no, I was *not* abused as a child. My childhood was highly sheltered, hopelessly protected. I was spoiled with an abundance of love.

I grew up on the 'Gold Coast' of Long Island, New York in an area called Sands Point. My father, who was self-employed, sold and installed *Magic Doors*, the ones where you step on the vinyl carpet and the glass doors open automatically. In some ways, perhaps, this is a metaphor for how my childhood felt: Doors magically opened for me. In the 1950s, Dad was the first to sell this brand new 'magic' door in the NY area, and by the time I was ten he had built his family and his business and purchased a 3-acre estate in Harbor Acres, a well-to-do neighborhood that fronted a small beach area on the Long Island Sound. Neighbors included the President of Mobil Oil, Perry Como and wealthy Wall Street brokers. Certain areas within Nassau and Suffolk Counties comprise 'the Gold Coast' where historic mansions dot beach areas from Oyster Bay to Sands Point, where F. Scott Fitzgerald was said to have written his *Great Gatsby*.

My memories of childhood were mostly sweet with a special closeness to my mother. I remember family road trips to the mountains or to the town next door to see Aunt

Renee and our cousins. I remember sleep-overs, jump rope, pogo sticks, ice skating and Sweet Sixteen parties. Mine was a childhood filled with good memories and bright, shiny impressions of almost *too* much. Always an abundance, always more than we could have imagined. With its slate patios, fish ponds and immaculate landscaping, my mostly idyllic upbringing was, if anything, secure.

Secure from the knowledge that sick monsters even existed.

Secure that children went to sleep at night safe in their beds.

Secure that no one would ever hurt me, nor break my soul.

*****

How many little souls did he break? How many families' lives had been destroyed? None of them could have known that Bradley's crimes would soon grow to include criminal charges that included the sexual exploitation and rape of 127 children at his practice or his home in Lewes, Delaware. For there is video evidence, hours and hours of it, mostly in 45-second clips taped by his own hand. Later, several months after his arrest, there would be over 500 charges against this one-time pediatrician who is currently incarcerated in the James T. Vaughn correctional facility in Smyrna, Delaware.

Perhaps as a child, a teenager and a young adult, because violent crimes didn't exist in my mind anyway, I became drawn to them. Just as I became a candy addict, because I couldn't have it as a little girl, I, would later become a true crime junkie. It's been that way since I fell in love with reading as a young adult. Drawn to stories about the ugly side of real life and crime, I devoured books like *Valley of the Dolls, Slaughterhouse Five* and the true account of *Patricia Hearst*. I loved authors like Ann Rule and read James A. Mitchener's *Drifters,* or the real-life story about war protesters shot and killed at Kent State. Fictional thrillers based in fact by authors like Michael Crichton or John Grisham and of course Capote's *In Cold Blood* are still my favorites. Later, I'd never miss a TV episode of *Dateline, Criminal Minds, Notorious* or *CSI* nor miss a book by Greg Iles, Keith Ablow or Nelson DeMille.

Grown-Up

In 1974, after graduating from Susquehanna University, I moved to Alexandria, Virginia with three college friends. We split the rent of an upscale two-bedroom apartment with its gold shag carpet and used furniture, got starter jobs and later, one by one, moved away for better jobs or marriage and kids. I was the only one who stayed in Northern Virginia, getting married at age thirty-two and divorcing in my early forty's. Still, I'd found a career I loved in the trade show production business. By fifty though, I knew the time had come to finally open my own business, something I'd wanted for twenty years. I also knew that if I could grow it to success, I'd be able to move the business and myself to Rehoboth Beach, Delaware.

I wanted to be near the ocean.

I wanted less traffic. I wanted no more rat race.

And I found it.

After searching for my new home for three years, living in Rehoboth was exactly as I'd dreamed. Now, as I sit in front of my lap top, in my library with its red-painted walls, in my home just two miles from the beach, I think of how, at age 56, I'd chosen small town living for a reason. When I moved to Rehoboth in December 2007, I felt welcomed and safe again – in the way I had been as a child. Until I settled in Rehoboth, I hadn't realized just how much I'd longed for a simpler way of life, worlds away from the Long Islands or the Fairfax, Virginias. I found it in Rehoboth where I became a part of 'beach living' quickly, with an article in the local Gazette newspaper about my business.

I felt a kind of pure delight like I'd never known. I volunteered for a local autism foundation, found new friends and discovered the type of writers' guild I'd dreamed of being a part of. In the mornings now, I often take my dogs for beach runs as seagulls dive for fish, kids fly red and purple-colored kites or dolphin fins peek through waves. Or I sit for hours at the Starbucks sipping a latte and reading local news tidbits. For the first time in my adult life, I felt a part of some *thing,* some *where.*

Southern Delaware

During 'off-season' most people know one another in this small town of fewer than 2000 year-round residents. You can't go to the grocery store, Starbucks or the vet without bumping into a friend or recognizing the waiter from your favorite restaurant. I love this.

I love that I can smell salt in the air.

I love the casual, *wear shorts all year round if you want*, kind of feeling.

I love that people are so friendly. And I love that people seem to take care of each other.

When I was recovering from knee surgery, neighbors helped me without my ever having to ask. People care too about protecting their natural resources. There are heated debates on the search for alternative forms of energy or organized walks to clean the beach. There is a particular pride here for an area that is alive with creative energy and a true passion for the arts. There is an annual jazz fest, film fest, Art festivals and literary readings. I even love the local news stories about MERR (The Marine Education, Rescue and Rehabilitation Institute) saving beached whales – and if they can't save them, they will study the whale to find out why it died on our shores.

This would be the world that Bradley hurt. In this town where I'd come to feel part of a community, what he did was beyond shocking, it was unthinkable. And when I first heard about his arrest just days before my second Christmas living at the beach, something in me crumbled and a piece of that idyllic feeling broke off.

It just fell away like the waves do as one washes beneath the next.

Somehow I'd become transfixed by a serial child molester.

Delmarva

Because so many of us know each other in these towns it's only natural to speak in hushed tones when scandal or tragedy touches our area. This is what we do here – we whisper, refusing to talk about the *bad* things out loud. Someone may over-react, someone will talk about you, someone who's been affected by the tragedy may overhear. Because so many were.

So sometimes, you act invisible. That's the way I felt as word of Bradley's case seeped, like an infection, throughout Sussex County.

Sussex County, Delaware is a part of a larger area or land mass commonly known as Delmarva, where beautiful beach towns speckle the coastline from Wilmington, Delaware through Virginia Beach. A large peninsula on the Eastern Coastline of the United States, it is occupied by the entire state of Delaware, and portions of Virginia and Maryland; hence, the acronym *Delmarva*. The peninsula is almost 180 x 60 miles and is bordered by the Chesapeake Bay on the West and the Delaware River, Delaware Bay and the Atlantic on the east. Out of fifty states only Rhode Island is smaller than Delaware.

Lewes

Present-day Lewes, (pronounced Lewis) is most well-known, amongst Delawareans as, "the first town in the first state in the nation" and traces its history back to 1631. A bronze plaque sits in front of a miniature brown lighthouse that commemorates this fact upon entering town. I can't help but think how lighthouses are historic symbols of safety and trust that mark dangerous coastlines, assuring a ship's safe entry into inland bays and harbors. Lewes is situated upon Delaware Bay which is the body of water between Cape May, New Jersey and the state of Delaware. The massive, bright-white, Cape May-Lewes ferry boats connect our shores and have since July 1964.

I can almost hear Otis Redding singing *Sittin' on the Dock of the Bay* as I watch the majestic ferries arrive and depart. The three deep blasts of the ships' horn signals last call for departure. Friends and relatives wave good-by as if the ships were leaving for Europe, when instead they are about to take the short 85-minute voyage over to Cape May, New Jersey. There is something romantic, something deeply reminiscent of olden days as I watch these car-carrying boats depart or enter port; the most dramatic part being the ships docking procedure as it swings, swivels and shimmies its bow around to back into its 'parking space.' Each time I watch these magnificent ships dock, I think of something the size of a football field maneuvering its way, so very gracefully into port – each time, this 'dock dance' reminds me of an elephant backing in to a hall foyer. The ship pushes and pulls, rocks back and forth rhythmically, when it finally snuggles into its slot some ten minutes later.

It is said the Cape May-Lewes Ferry terminal in Lewes is haunted. I learned that 800 souls were lost at sea; their bodies washed up near the location and whose ghosts still roam the property late at night. Visible evidence of those souls lost is the Unknown Sailors' Cemetery marker along the terminal dock, placed in memory of the "hundreds of sailors who lost their lives and whose unidentified bodies were here cast ashore."

Ghost stories, abound in Lewes. I love hearing of "strange occurrences" happening right here in my new home town.

I've heard reports of a white 'figure' moving in the area of the terminals sunroom – it was supposedly recorded on two cameras.

Other stories have circulated among ferry employees over the years about unexplained encounters. Some heard loud crying in the storage area when no one else was working; other early morning employees have reported seeing a man in a cape with long white hair. "He walked into the women's restroom but there was no one in there." Later the strong odor of cigar smoke was detected in the restroom. It is said the same entity has been seen walking the streets of Lewes.

I'll usually visit downtown Lewes after watching the ferries. There is something about Lewes. Something I can't describe adequately, enough. What I do know is that somehow I am filled with delight, even warmth in the middle of winter when I venture downtown. Lewes: With its quaint red brick sidewalks, flower-boxed, lantern lit, bench-lined streets. Lewes: With the unusual and ancient architecture of its churches, it's maritime museums and chic boutiques. The fighting lion and blue and gold checkerboard Coat of Arms shield of Lewes, East Sussex England (the original Lewes coat of arms) waves from Town Hall. This coat of arms is also emblazoned on the sleeves of Lewes Police uniforms and flies from flagpoles, fire department vehicles and is engraved into original building structures. Its origins date back over a thousand years to the Norman Conquest; this is a town fiercely proud of its heritage and history.

History abounds in the towns' restored and relocated historic homes. The Ryves Holt House is recognized as the oldest building in the entire state. Built in 1665, it stands on its original site at the corner of Second and Mulberry, its newest "Spanish" brown/red color most likely duplicating its early color during the 1600s. A bronze tablet acquaints visitors with the prominent resident of Ryves Holt Esq (1696-1763) who lived in the home from age 25 to his death, which took his body only a few paces from his homes' doorstep to its final resting place at St. Peter's churchyard. The epitaph on his grave tells of his amiable nature and states that in life, "his benevolent disposition endeared him to his friends."

The quaint Maull House is another of Lewes' many historic structures. Built by a carpenter named Samuel Paynter in a section of Lewes known as Pilot Town, the houses here were originally owned by officers performing maritime duties. Many of these were members of the pioneering Maull family: Patriots, pilots, shipbuilders and farmers. From its creek-front perch, the early inhabitants could view the Delaware Bay and the Cape Henlopen Lighthouse. It is here where a local, romantic legend seems to have permanently moved into the home. Apparently Jerome Bonaparte, brother of Napoleon, and his bride, Betsy, found refuge on a stormy night in 1803, when their ship docked into Lewes Harbor for repairs. Betsy, of the wealthy Patterson family of Baltimore, is still remembered for refusing to be seated at a bounteous roast goose dinner until her silver candlesticks had been brought from the disabled ship.

Sixty years ago Lewes in summer was a bustling town. Most of the visitors were not tourists, but seasonal fishermen and boat captains. Fish factories dotted the shoreline along Delaware Bay and sometimes the smell was dreadful. Some compare this smell to burnt fish or some kind of awful decay. Fishing fueled the towns' economy with Lewes leading the way as the number one fishing port in the country in the mid-1950s. Just ten years later, the fish factories closed and the workers were gone. The demise of the industry would transform Lewes from a working-class fishing town into a trendy tourist one.

Lewes has a special and hard won history behind it, where perseverance and strength triumphed over adversity. There is a certain pride in living here. One story of the first town in the first state dates back to Christmas Eve 1673 when 40 armed horsemen thundered into the area. In a battle for control between the English and the Dutch over the region, the Governor, Charles Calvert, told his men to go to the area and "devastate the settlement there." The Governor gave orders to the Captain to collect all arms, seize all boats, gather all the people from the countryside into the area of Lewes and within minutes of the warning, burn all buildings to the ground.

The townspeople were unable to stop the ruthless destruction of their town. Only one thatch barn remained standing after this tragedy.

Unable to defend themselves, destitute people bonded together and began to rebuild their town.

Just as they do today.

This fierce tenacity remains strong as the citizenry of Lewes fight to maintain their historic roots. They will often reject commercial growth to maintain the town's charm and quaint 'little town by the sea' image. In 2008 when a commercial realtor with deep social and political roots attempted to construct a town center near the high school, complete with condominiums, shops and 'lovely treed park areas' the townspeople banded together again. They formed a foundation. They formed committees and they instituted town meeting after town meeting. Full page editorials condemned the new structure in local papers. Signs on almost every front lawn read "Lewes is not for Sale!" And "Not in Our Town!" Those signs stayed on those lawns for years. All the while Dr. Earl Bradley continued to build his pediatric business one mile west of downtown. By the time the commercial project was defeated in early 2010, and the signs removed, the slogan "not in our town" would have a far more sinister implication.

Today Lewes is consistently ranked #1 in the Best Places to Live annual survey in the magazine *Delaware Today*. Why? "Well," as the article says "Who wouldn't want to live here? Quaint homes, an appreciation of history, the beautiful nature park of Cape Henlopen, longtime residents that maintain a real small-town vibe, an active Little League that plays on prime canal-front property, great shopping and dining and excellent schools. Enough said."

Beach-Life

The Southern half of Delaware is known as "Lower, Slower Delaware" or LSD as seen on car decals, by the locals. Everything and everyone moves at a slower pace. People would rather be fishing, hunting, painting or walking on the beach. That's just the way it is, that is, until June when

Lewes and its neighboring beach town of Rehoboth where I live, change drastically. These beach towns collectively swell to well over 150,000 during the summer months. This is when tens of thousands from the mid-Atlantic region and as far north as New York visit our shores.

Residents who live at the beach year-round often find themselves in a heightened state of anticipation. Waiting for the excitement of summer with its boardwalk, rides at Funland, Louie's' Pizza, Thrasher's Fries and Dolle's salt water taffy; they wait for the community events of fall, like the film fest, a premier showing of artistic films which had not been generally released to the public but films that had won awards. There's Jazz fest where hundreds come from out of state to listen to visiting musicians play their instruments and sing all over town and then there's Sea Witch Festival that celebrates Halloween in grand tradition with parades, children's games and costumes all over town. This is the period of time after the summer crowds dwindle and locals take the reins again. From the "Talk of Delmarva" local (very local) radio station of WGMD 92.7 to the popular Tanger outlets, beach life here, is quite simply, very different than anywhere else.

Considered upscale and wealthy, the towns of Rehoboth and Lewes boast well-known art galleries, live theatre, superb eateries, soft sandy beaches, artsy boutiques, and sparkling clean boardwalks. I love the 'flip-flop' bright white benches that line the mile long boardwalk in Rehoboth. I'll often flip the back of the bench to watch the waves or flip it again to watch and listen to local school-inspired musicals performed at the bandstand. Rehoboth's symbol, a bronze statue of a porpoise dances on its tail just behind the bandstand.

In Springtime, the shop keepers open their doors and windows wide as they clean and rid their stores of winter's cold and dust. The galleries get a fresh coat of paint, the restaurants and fish mongers return to begin again when spring brings back those who seemed lost during the long winter months. In the summer, children frolic at the seashore,

where clean, sun-sparkling water laps the sand.

Where children squeal with delight.

Families build sand castles, walk the board-walk and eat ice cream cones.

This is life at the beach.

A life that is about family, community, friendship and *trust*.

Until Dr. Earl Bradley.

Curiosity

I'd always, by nature, been extremely curious, almost to a fault. As a child, apparently I nearly drove my mother crazy with my questions of *why*....always "*why?*" – way beyond what my brother or sister would ask. Once, a long time ago, she told me she'd had a dream where she was trying to save me from our burning house and she kept screaming "get out, get out!" And I just stood there asking "But why, Mom? Why?"

Her dream got me to quit asking *why* all the time but I still felt it inside. And I still feel it - more so, since the story of Dr. Bradley broke in December 2009. I could not, for the life of me, understand the how or why of this case, nor could I comprehend why it took so long to stop him.

Why?

Appalled

How could there have been so many suspicions, so many red flags for <u>fourteen</u> years and each investigation was dropped, each innuendo ignored, each child damaged?

Again, I'd ask *Why*?

Or *How*?

From the moment I hear about Bradley's arrest I am appalled yet intrigued. Is it simply morbid curiosity? I think not – not when I see how this small town mystery grew more and more interesting, more and more bizarre. I become immersed in learning about Earl Bradley's background, understanding the legalities surrounding the case, understanding small town 'think' and mostly struggling to understand the man himself. I find myself researching every last detail of the Bradley case. I scour the *Wilmington News Journal,* listen intently for a mention of his name in the local *Cape Gazette*, WBOC and ABC news broadcasts, and scan the internet for more clues. I read books like *Secret Survivors* by Susan Blume, Keith Ablow's *Psychopath*, and *The Trauma Myth* by Susan Clancy, *Pedophiles and Predators* and *the Sociopath Next Door*. I sit in my car for hours on a grey fall afternoon starring at Bradley's now defunct, run-down place of business. On another afternoon I visit the hospital where he'd worked, then spend an hour sitting across from his now-deserted home. I read about his addictions to alcohol, pain killers and mood enhancers - and I try to grapple with mental disorders yet to be diagnosed like borderline personality disorder, pedophilia, extreme depression, sexual sadism and bi-polar illness.

Through all of this I grapple with the question people continually asked: "Why are <u>you</u> doing this?" As the months wear on, it becomes a question I ask myself over and over. I want to believe that perhaps within this process, I'll come to understand something about evil.

About human nature.

About inhumanity.

About compassion.

Perhaps I would also learn about forgiveness, that sometimes, some things – are simply unforgivable.

Maybe I will learn about our capacity to damage and maybe, too, about people's capacity to survive. Finally, perhaps I will come to understand the nature of secrets and silence and about how dangerous they can be. And somewhere in all of this I hope to find strength: that even though I hadn't been personally damaged by Bradley, I still have the right to tell this story as I see it.

Or to tell it at all.

For this story, like many, is about missed opportunities:

Medical personnel and law enforcement missed the opportunity to stop him.

They missed the opportunity to educate the children – and the families on child abuse.

Still considered by most to be a shameful, dirty little secret that is not spoken of, even medical personnel missed the opportunity and didn't see the signs to stop a pedophile living in their midst.

There were missed opportunities to *help* the children.

There was even *his* missed opportunity to develop a healthy, productive or normal life.

I didn't want to miss what has come to be my opportunity - *my* responsibility to tell this story. In the end, it is about one man. A pediatrician, who once specialized in the medical care of children.

It is a story of betrayal, despair and evil.

It is a story of the monster known as Dr. Earl Bradley and it is the story of my obsession with his story.

Beginning

This is how it all begins. "A Lewes pediatrician turned himself in on Friday December 18, after being charged with 26 counts related to the sexual abuse of female patients ranging in age from three months to thirteen years old," police said. Counts include first-degree rape, second degree rape and fourteen counts of sexual exploitation of a child by film and endangering the welfare of a child – all felonies.

Dr. Earl Bradley, 56, who operated Baybees Pediatrics, is originally held on bail in the amount of $36,000. After police raid his practice and seize computer and digital recording equipment that helped identify victims, Bradley will be held on nearly $3 million cash bail.

Although this is huge and the number – 26 counts – awful, it is only the beginning. Soon enough, the police will uncover graphic video files showing Bradley molesting and raping children. A veteran forensic investigator said the series of video clips, some lasting 45 seconds, others up to 15 minutes, "These were some of the most violent and brutal attacks on a child of any age, he'd ever seen."

"*Ever*?" I ask myself. A feeling of gut-twisting sadness washes through me.

Dr. Bradley is immediately suspended from Beebe Medical Center where he was allowed medical privileges and was on staff. He will later lose his medical license.

Damage

My bedroom feels cold as I sit on the side of my bed listening to the broadcasts. Was it the temperature of the house or hearing more about the case that makes me feel chilled? All I know, just a week before Christmas, is that I am going to write about this and that the story would be *my* account as I watch it, as I feel it. I know a gag order had been issued. And I know I can't 'impede an ongoing case' by asking questions of the prosecution or Bradley himself, of families impacted, of the hospital – of anyone - so I have to confine my search to reading everything I can: Countless articles and Google alerts, books and magazine articles on true crime and pedophilia, blogs, editorials. I'd have to dive headfirst into this ocean of research and finally – once I'd done this – I'd have to surface and face the people in this very small town, who might not like the fact I'd decided to write this story.

In the first town, in the first state of Delaware, who would have ever thought that there would soon be hundreds of child molestation counts against Bradley;

that hundreds of families would be irrevocably damaged,

that a doctor had been investigated and/or under suspicion for fourteen years but that no one would take action, legal or otherwise, against him.

Who would have ever thought there could be so many secrets in such a small town?

Hell

Bradley's practice sits on prime real estate just off Route One next to the Community Bank off Kings Highway which leads to 'Old Town,' Lewes. It's just a mile or so to Beebe Medical Center. For years, those who didn't go to Dr. Bradley thought his practice was some kind of day care or baby-sitting service. With its miniature Ferris wheel, its 2nd 'out-house' type building painted in black and white checker-boards, and life-size Buzz Lightyear on the front lawn, it looked like a kiddie's playground.

But it was messy. It wasn't like any other medical office that anyone had ever seen before. Something sinister had been happening at Baybees Pediatrics for years.

What was Dr. Bradley's reality? How distorted had it grown? He appeared to exist in a world of make-believe – of bumble bees and Disney land flights of fancy, of Broadway plays and super human comic characters. But what must the inner chatter in his head have been like?

I try to picture him before he violated a child. Did he ever question what he was about to do? Did he ever wonder why? Was he unbearably tense or were his actions snap judgments that sprang from a damaged psyche?

As I gaze out my kitchen window, mindlessly washing dishes, I imagine that Disney song, "It's a Small World" might be playing on his Bose stereo system. *It's a world of laughter, a world of tears - It's a world of hope, and a world of fears...* might be heard in the waiting room or in a Mermaid-themed exam room. When I force myself to see him, I know that not even the playful music relieves the doctor of his urges. When these urges overtook him, his skin must have been hot with angst. The palms of his hands red with sweat. He might grip the examination room's counter top that holds his sink, scrip pads and assorted tools of his trade.

Did his heart pound?

Or did he calmly hum alongside ...*it's a small world after all*.

Jabbing the dishes into the dishwasher now, I imagine his brain throbbing inside his head, just before taking *them* to the basement for a popsicle or Disney doll.

Them: The younger children

Them: The six-month old babies

Them: The helpless; the ones who could not yet speak, the most vulnerable.

In his reality, did he ever try to fight it? His breathing would come faster now. Did he try to slow down his breathing as he wiped sweat from his forehead?

His Practice

I can picture his practice and exam rooms. Based on articles I read on his escalating illnesses and how unclean his life had become, I can picture a thin film of dust and grime that might cover the tops of computers or desk accessories in his office. Perhaps the faint odor of Lysol or disinfectant or bleach covered up the stink that came from dirty scrubs, speckled floors or unchanged exam table coverings. In the tiny kitchenette, the top of the refrigerator had probably never been cleaned. Grimy dishes and coffee cups might have sat in the sink for days.

And the reader might stop me here asking, "How could parents continue to bring their kids to him if he, his office, was so dirty?" My answer would be twofold. Initially, he was a gifted doctor who went above and beyond, feigning devotion to their child. He was also a gifted groomer of both the parents and children. And perhaps, in later years those parents became so devoted to him, they didn't notice the changes in Bradley's messy appearance or his more bizarre way of behaving; or maybe they dismissed their uneasy second-thoughts, telling themselves they were being silly, imagining something that wasn't really there.

So, I'd say to those who'd ask this question...*he wasn't always like that.*

Later on in the years that followed 2004, 2005, most who visited his office to interview him found him odd, not quite right – and they usually didn't stick around. Additionally, by then, there were more pediatricians to choose from. But in the 1990's there were only a few pediatricians in this area. These are rural seaside towns after all.

Ah, but those surveillance cameras. The ones, said to be in every exam room, were probably spotless – when all around his practice seemed to rein chaos and disorder. Did he sneak back in after work to clean them? Clearly, as I would later learn at trial, *they* were his most prized possessions.

Headlines

On my desk is a file filled with over one hundred articles, the headlines alone telling the facts of the story. Even now, as I skim through my stack of articles I think that this is only the beginning.

On December 16: Lewes Doctor arrested on felony charges

On December 22 Charges Mount in Lewes Pediatrician Case;

January 5: Lewes Doc Could Face Life in Prison;

Followed by, Police Affidavit lists Eight Alleged victims.

The headlines come one after another that January - each one, another chapter in the story: And then, another blow in January: *Bradley Tested for HIV.*

The growing case was inescapable - on the radio, in newspapers, TV and on the tip of everyone's tongue. Milford Police Investigated Bradley in '05; Bradley Victims Could Number over 100; Bradley Victims Come Together."

The next month, February 2010, Bradley's medical license was revoked and the state and medical societies would begin their independent investigations. On February 23rd the headline reads: *Grand Jury Indicts Bradley on 471 counts.* The counts include everything from rape to sexual exploitation of a child. The numbers have soared from 8 children to over 100, from 39 counts to 471. Taking a deep breath, I let the number sink in:

471.

More days than there are in a year.

471.

I can't get my head around this number or begin to describe my reaction.

Surprise?

No, surprise is not the right word when I see the number 471 for surprise is too happy of a word.

A word that reminds me of birthday parties or celebrations.

Almost 500 counts against 100 children.

471. On average, five counts per child.

Incredulous? No. I think not for this word is still not enough.

Unbelievable is not the right word either because the number 471 is true – it must be believed – it is documented on video by his own hand.

I suppose the word horrified would be the right one to describe my reaction to this ugly number – a number I know, will grow.

On WBOC's local News that same night, Attorney General Beau Biden asks "how did this physician remain in our midst for so long?" He is wide-eyed and appears stunned. I know he has two young children of his own. The indictment packet is as large and as heavy as a novel, 160 pages of multiple crimes committed by one doctor. The indictment comes after the Attorney General's office has had the time to review the fourteen hours of video taped evidence. 14 hours. The national news media goes crazy: From Katie Courick and CNN to Dr. Phil and *The Washington Post*, suddenly everyone wants to report the story.

By the time the warmer breezes of springtime finally hit, and when summer slides into fall, the number *does* grow to 529. With new indictments against him, with new victims coming forward, they appear to march, every month, single file, one by one into the Attorney General's satellite office near the hospital where Bradley worked, one block from his home. This satellite office, with its wooden exterior and freshly painted shutters sits next door to the Beebe Medical Center and has been rented for the State Justice Department staff. Mainly, these state department employees are there to help, to counsel affected families; the office is there for the state investigators who spend hundreds of hours identifying the children in the videos taken from Bradley's home and practice.

As the families come forward, the charges against him mount, like a mountain building itself out of molten rock, like bricks piling atop one another to create a tall building.

If I can't wrap my head around the number 471, it is no wonder I feel sucker-punched when on March 3 the paper reads: Dr. Earl Bradley Sex Case Ignites Outrage. It's sub title: *Indictment says abuse was so harsh five girls appear to pass out*. During this same month one of the headlines blasts: Bradley pleads Not Guilty! *On April 20 Bradley to Face Second trial on 58 New Charges*.

My stack of newspapers on the Bradley case rises a foot off the floor in my little red library by now - four months since his arrest, the number of children he violated has grown ten-fold. All the while I keep asking myself how can this be.

Parents

Before the arrest, there were different schools of thought about the doctor who buzzed around town in his bright yellow 'bumblebee' Volkswagen. To some he was a messy oddball, socially awkward, overly flamboyant. To others, including many medical professionals who took their own kids to his practice, he was a talented doctor with a gift for relating to children.

Yet, for the great majority of the parents who trusted Dr. Bradley and brought their child to see him, most of them couldn't have known – would never have thought to mistrust their child's pediatrician. This is because Bradley was so good at manipulating the parents.

Still, even though people learned in the months after his arrest, how diabolically cunning he was, many would ask "Where were the parents?" The question reverberated in my head. Four ordinary words I couldn't let go of. "Where were the parents?" I'm not sure why these words infuriated me so. It's a valid question, I suppose. *Where were the parents?* And yet each time I heard it, as I drove to Starbucks in the mornings, as I sat at my desk working on a project, or as I stood at the counter slicing cucumbers for a salad, I heard the question in my mind and felt again that knot of anger in my gut. *Where were the parents?*

Today, just days after those infamous blizzards of 2010, I am driving home from the grocery store, over huge ice bumps and poorly plowed roads; our transportation department has never had snow like these back-to-back blizzards. The plows can't keep up with over two feet of the white stuff. Consequently, I drive the half mile home almost hitting my head on the roof of the car with every jarring pot hole or ice bump, thinking how there are still so many questions about Bradley. They are everywhere. They swirl like the snow has for weeks.

"Why didn't the office personnel at Baybees (his medical practice) notice the video equipment?"

How could it have gone on so long?"

"How can any lawyer in Delaware defend this man?"

"How could everyone have known him so well and not really know him at all? He played Santa Claus on the Christmas parade float for Christ's sake."

All valid questions. But the more troubling one is "Where were the parents?" And "How could anyone leave their child alone like that?"

I wonder how impossible it must be for the victims' parents to hear these questions again and again. How do they shield their children, themselves, from talk of the case, which saturates local media and sidewalk gossip.

No matter how much these parents are told not to feel guilty, *not* to listen to the news and gossipy neighbors, the parents of these children must feel massive guilt and grave shame that they hadn't been able to protect their child. One father recently forced himself to hold his tongue when he was standing in line in front of two strangers who were gossiping about the case. At Dick's Sporting Goods, the strangers heaped blame on "those kids' parents." The father wanted to whirl around and say, "If that monster could fool me, he could fool you." The father told reporters. "You hear that stuff, it's like an arrow in your heart."

Again, I think of their heartache and *that* question with its implied judgment. It seems to be the first thing any of the non-victims ask. And really, the question could pertain to any of a dozen similar situations. Any situation where a child is left unprotected. And these 'Bradley' children were, weren't they?

Unprotected?

I think of other situations: A child accidentally drowns in a pool out back in the split second his mother turns away, but still it is asked, where was his mother? Or a child wanders off in a Walmart, gets lost and people wonder how it could happen – wasn't the mother watching him? Or even when a child is alone in a hospital room and you think where are his parents? How could anyone leave him by himself here in this impersonal, cold room? A question I might have asked or thought in tons of other situations.

Why then, am I so angry now?

I know it's because of the blame that is insinuated every time the question is asked. I know that *Where were the parents* really means i*t's the parent's fault for letting this happen.* I know *where were the parents* is another way of saying *this wouldn't have happened to my child – I wouldn't let it happen.* This self-righteous attitude is what makes me furious. But after the anger, my mind tries to analyze it. I wonder about parents needing to believe that they can *always* protect their child. Are these statements or questions, really self-righteousness or are those who make them, simply terrified that this too could happen to them and the implied judgment is some kind of bravado – something to hide their own fears?

Still the talk and innuendo only adds to parents' pain. Strangers, bloggers, even friends, blame the parents for being seemingly careless – for not protecting their children against the likes of Earl Bradley.

"Why the hell did those parents leave their kids alone with him? Who does that," one blogger asks. I tell myself he couldn't have known all the facts.

Continually, I find myself standing up for those parents. My outcry for them, perhaps, tends to go overboard when my sense of injustice feels challenged by those who throw blame around too easily.

Still I tell the facts again and again in defense of the parents who trusted Bradley. They couldn't have known when he whisked their child off to the prize room, that this was where he'd rape them, sometimes in less than four minutes. In some of the videos he himself had taken, it happened in 45 seconds. *45 seconds* is incomprehensible to me. 45 seconds – less time than it takes to heat a cup of tea in the morning; less time than it takes to brush your teeth at night. And sometimes the parent sat in the very exam room where Bradley groped or touched their children. His cameras were everywhere - Aside from the wall-mounted cameras, he even managed to use a small surveillance camera hidden in an ordinary pen that he'd lay on the exam table.

Devious.

Unthinkable. Sometimes he positioned himself between the parent and her child so the parent had trouble seeing. One parent shifted her position so she could see around Bradley, to keep her child in view. As she was repositioning herself, the doctor reportedly inserted two fingers into the child's vagina. The child screamed. When the parent confronted him, the doctor laughed it off, called the parent silly, used intimidation tactics that usually worked so that the parent second-guessed herself and once again, no police report, no medical board report.

I'm almost home now, going about 10 miles per hour in 40 mph speed zone over these frozen roads. As I pull into my driveway I wonder why I feel like the only person who doesn't ask the question about the parents – about where they were.

Then I think, these parents who *can't* understand, ask "How could the parents not have known?" I ask "How could they?"

Doubts

As the deep winter sun filtered through Lewes' quaint turn-of-the-century buildings, the horror of children being raped by a local, well-respected doctor filtered through the town. Dr. Earl Bradley found and groomed both his young patients and their parents for more than fourteen years. By grooming I mean this is what child predators do to their victims. This is usually how they are able to get away with it for so long. First they befriend them, feign interest, showing they care greatly for the child. Once the parents' trust is gained, the predator begins to prey. Why, then, once parents are properly groomed, would they dream of mistrusting the predator?

I am trying to keep up with all the articles that come one after the other in our newspapers. Daily, we learn more details. Still, when I see the word pedophile and pediatrician in the same sentence, I have to read and re-read that sentence. Again and again, it just doesn't register as I sit on a stool, bent over the speckled island counter top in my kitchen.

These news stories about Bradley unfolded slowly in articles, on TV, on local talk radio. The stories increased in intensity, as did the reaction, the disbelief and even the denial. It would be the main topic talked about on sidewalks, in stores, almost everywhere.

What's more, state officials, the local medical society, medical personnel, doctors and law enforcement were made aware of Bradley's actions as early as 1998 but they failed to stop him. The resulting carnage, the fallout, has swept through our small beach towns like an unending tidal wave.

Dr. Phil

The March 4 broadcast of the Dr. Phil Show does a segment about Bradley called: *When the System Fails.*

I've watched The Dr. Phil Show for years now. Rarely have I seen him so frustrated. So angry. The show begins with Dr. Phil standing center stage in front of a large TV screen and a still photo of Bradley's mug shot above a picture of his pediatrics practice. Dr. Phil asks, "How would you feel if your child was molested by your doctor even when he was on the radar of Attorney General, other doctors, and under investigation and you were never told? You were allowed to walk your child right in there and put your child in his hands," Dr. Phil points to the new photo of

Bradley being led away in hand-cuffs, hair askew; he looks like a wild man.

I am riveted as Dr. Phil relates the story of Earl Bradley to his audience – his sentences seem to meld together:

> *System failures affect us all.... worst serial offender of all time.... prosecutors say worst single assault and rape of one hundred children....videotaped attacks took less than 45 seconds....gained parents' trust....lured children away....muzzled some of the children....if they'd only known.*

Nancy Grace, host of The Nancy Grace Show on CNN and a mother of twins says "I feel sick and I feel angry." Dr. Phil almost seems to be goading Nancy; inciting her with questions that provoke her making her more and more angry. Good for TV ratings, I suppose.

> *"How were these young children allowed to be taken away from their parents and why wasn't there anyone else in the room?" asks Nancy.*

Dr. Phil explains how the parents trusted him and sometimes he'd take the children to the prize room for a few brief moments. How, sometimes, Bradley touched the children inappropriately when parents were in the very same room.

"Freak!" a red-faced Nancy shouts at the camera.

The story Dr. Phil presents keeps getting worse, although by now I'd read much of it in the newspapers:

Nancy: "You assume that when a state licenses a doctor they do a check. How does a system break down this bad?

How do we...how do those parents get justice? I don't want to put parents on a guilt trip but who lets their child go with a doctor alone for a vaginal exam?"

I am jolted almost out of my seat. My head whips back as if being struck. How dare she ask this question on national television I ask out loud. I am furious at Dr. Phil and Nancy for the way this show is coming across. Maybe I'm too close to it but I'm feeling so angry my nerve ends actually feel tingly, as if they are buzzing. Why, I ask myself then, am I so angry *again*? Is it because I, myself have not yet accepted the fact that the system *had* let down so many families so horribly? Have I been focused so ferociously on Bradley that I haven't really focused on how the system itself failed? Is it heartbreak I'm feeling or outrage that what Dr. Phil and Nancy Grace seem to be doing is sensationalizing just about everything? Or is it really, because they are saying the truth and I don't want to believe it. I wonder what other viewers in Delaware think as they watch this show. I'm thinking the parents must feel hurt by it especially when Nancy dares to ask that horrible question again, about *where were the parents?*.

Dr. Phil takes the viewing audience through an entire timeline of when Bradley first came under suspicion and asks "How in the world could it take so long to stop him?" He explains that "Bradley hit the radar in 2004, 2005 2008, 2009." Then asks again "Why did it take so long to get a warrant?" He goes on to explain that there was no probable cause to move forward and the state police originally involved were "incompetent." Why didn't the medical board, the medical society, or someone come to the police?

Why didn't they work together?" His eyes are open wide. He is waving his arms as if to pull the audience into his disgust, his own outrage, at how so many balls were dropped.

How every suspicion, every investigation was dropped.

How no one really did anything to stop him. For years.

Near the end of the show Dr. Phil asks, "Nancy, what can parents do to protect their children?" Nancy appears to have calmed somewhat since Dr. Phil's explanations. She seems sad now, less severe and angry. Her eyes well. She must be thinking of her own two young children I think. But then the anger is back. Gritting and showing her bright white TV teeth, she almost growls into the camera's lens, "Don't leave your children alone, ever, with anyone."

"Agreed, Nancy." Dr. Phil replies "This pervert kept videos. They were probably dated and stamped. I just wish the judge had granted that original warrant."

Nancy's anger returns in full force. "It all makes my blood boil. Why didn't the medical board make a move? They were protecting their own." No, I think. This statement has my blood boiling. No one could have known how far he'd gone. They would have done something...anything, if they had any idea!

Wouldn't they? I ask.

"Trust your gut. Learn from this – DON'T leave your children alone, ever." The camera zooms in for a tight shot. Even as he finishes the show, Dr. Phil appears aghast, shocked, surprised at his own report. The show's themed music quietly plays in the background. The viewing audience knows the show is coming to an end. I feel wired. I am still seething when Dr. Phil closes the segment with the quote, "All you need for evil to prevail is for good men to stand by and do nothing."

Not only am I feeling anger, but for some reason, I *think* I am feeling shame. Why? Because the system *did* fail? Because it happened here, in my lovely, new home town? Because the Dr. Phil show aired our dirty laundry on national television? But it is all true. Even though it will take me many more months to understand this and to come to terms with it all. The doctors, the medical society, law enforcement, the hospital – it, the system, all failed these children and their families.

The state of Delaware imposes a gag order a few weeks after the show airs. The national news coverage on Dr. Bradley soon comes to a halt. Local coverage doesn't.

Broken

Months after the Dr. Phil Show, I read that Delaware trails only second to Mississippi as the state least likely to discipline doctors when complaints are made against them. Did Bradley know this when he moved to Lewes?

The failure of doctors, hospitals and medical staffers to inform the law, the Board of Medical Practice or Child Protective Services (CPS) allowed the pediatrician to continue sexually abusing children for years.

Part II: Spring 2010

Delmarva is a unique and wonderful place. It's one not defined by its cities or towns. Delmarva is a bond, created by geography and strengthened by family and by history. It is a long history of bountiful harvest by church dotted landscapes; a history that's seen triumph over adversity. Our land has changed as the world has changed. And storms that cross our great nation sometimes pass through here. But here we remain, one place, one people and here we will keep and protect the most precious part of all creation... our beloved children. The rest we must leave to a higher power.

From TV Special Bless Our Children, Protect Our Children,

Air date: WBOC, January, 2010, three weeks after the arrest.

The Children

On this warm April morning, the fog rolls in, erasing the landscape and even the house next door. It is a good day to stay indoors away from the gloom. Before Google-ing Child Abuse Prevention Month I want to learn more about the history of child abuse. As usual, I am curious. But what I find surprises me to the point where I'm mumbling out loud to myself.

I had no idea, for instance, that in the 1800s, tens of thousands of children were worked almost to death, were treated worse than animals and that *this* is where our child labor laws originated.

I find that in the 1800s in England 5-year olds worked 16 hour days in factories while shackled in chains – sometimes being whipped to work harder. Child abuse has existed and flourished throughout history in almost every culture, everywhere. Historically, two *rights* were at the core of violence against children: The right to own property and the right to *own* children.

I learn that sexual abuse within the family has always existed in spite of its taboo.

I learn too that parents used their children for labor or for profit more than a century ago.

The First Child Abuse Case

I had never heard of Mary-Ellen Wilson whose story is considered the very first child abuse case in North America. Scrolling down the page I shake my head at what I read: Until 1874, *animals were protected but children were not*. I read further, my heart aching and soaring at the same time, to learn about Mary-Ellen and Etta Wheeler.

It was 1873. Mary-Ellen Wilson was 9 years old when a church worker, Etta Wheeler, visited the Wilson's home and found Mary-Ellen shackled to her bed, grossly malnourished and badly beaten. Mrs. Wheeler went to the authorities but they turned her away. She did not give up. Instead she petitioned the American Society for the Prevention of Cruelty to Animals (ASPCA.) She asked them again and again to help Mary-Ellen. The ASPCA finally intervened to protect Mary-Ellen. The young girl was removed from her abusive home and placed in a foster care where she thrived. She went on to marry, have two daughters, and live to the age of 92.

Just as it is today with the Bradley case, several people tried to intervene; it bothers me that no one, at first, helped Mrs. Wheeler just as no one stopped Bradley. The authorities, the hospital, even the medical society had their own agendas. As a result, the suspicions, even the eye witness stories against Bradley, were dismissed for one reason and another. No one listened, just as they hadn't listened to Etta Wheeler.

130 years ago, when there were no laws to save Mary-Ellen, a group that protected the animals stepped in to save her. Her case led to the founding in 1874 of the Society of Prevention of Cruelty to Children- SPCC. It would be another eighty years until the advent of radiology and X-rays would be able to prove non-accidental injuries and actual child abuses.

I wonder what makes people like Etta Wheeler refuse to give up. Where did her strength come from?

I am surprised to learn Mary-Ellen's story; a little more surprised I'd never heard about her before. I dive head first into Google to see what else I can learn and I stumble upon a book written about Mary-Ellen called *Out of the Darkness,* the story of how the American Humane

Association, founded in 1877, had been born out of Mary-Ellen's and Etta Wheeler's dramatic case history. I race to my Kindle to order *Out of the Darkness*. On the cover of the book stands a wisp of a child. Her right hand grasps a French style, high back chair as if it supports her from falling. She wears a white, tattered dress. It is dirty. The picture is so stark, so real, I can feel her tears, her broken eyebrows, the permanent frown, the cuts and bruises that together tell her story of abuse.

I don't like this. Her picture tells so much more than I am able to describe. I feel inadequate even trying. What I really want to say is that there is something about her eyes, something forlorn, something hopeless. Like she has been forgotten; like she is nothing in this world.

It has grown dark in my library and Mary Ellen's picture is cast in shadow now. Insecurity washes through me like water through cracked glass. I am simply not good enough to describe her just as sometimes I feel like I'm not good enough to describe all the horror that is Earl Bradley . I walk outdoors to my deck where I stretch, thinking that maybe after I read the book, I will have a better feeling for Mary-Ellen. Then I will be able to bring justice to her story.

I think about one person's actions, or inaction, and how this can have a huge impact on so many. How the Society to protect children was born out of the same premise to *not* abuse animals. Again I am struck by Etta Wheeler's tenacity and I wonder what would have happened to Bradley had there been just one Etta Wheeler today.

I stop to make soup for lunch, all the while thinking of the computer. Why could Etta not let this go? One hundred and sixty years later shouldn't it be easier to save abused children?

I think of the two people who did try to stop Bradley. His half-sister Lynda Barnes back in 2005 and a nurse at Beebe hospital in 1995, who both told hospital authorities about Bradley's sometimes bizarre and unprofessional behaviors. If only they'd gone to the police. If only they'd gone to the state Medical <u>Board</u> and not the State <u>Society</u>. Would the medical board, which is responsible for licensing doctors and disciplining those doctors who break laws, have stopped Bradley? If only his sister, the nurse and so many others early on, had fought as hard as Etta Wheeler had.

If only.

Awareness

April is Child Abuse Prevention Month. It is also National Autism Awareness Month. I have often wondered who decides that this month or that would be dedicated to a specific cause, like the need to protect the children; or the need to increase awareness about autism. How do these random declarations come to be? Who proclaims the 'disease of the month?'

Searching for information about the various months dedicated to this cause or that, I land on a page that lists all the different prevention or awareness months or weeks and am shocked to find not just ten or twenty but literally hundreds: Burn Awareness day, National Condom Week, National School Breakfast Week – or the best yet, National Root Canal Week. "Are they kidding?" I shout out loud. I find that May has the highest number of these 'awareness' days: Better Sleep Month and Clean Air and Healthy Vision Week. It all seems so frivolous – National Ask Day? *Seriously*, I ask? I suppose these days and weeks mean something to someone but to proclaim them as a national 'day or week' still seems silly. A waste of resources for Congress to spend time on. And why? To appease a small group of people that work for a sleep association or a birth control association? I suppose, it is a question of politics and money and who has more of each.

I feel an unease, a discomfort, about the frivolous days or weeks even being mentioned in the same month as a proclamation for heart health, autism or child abuse. Still I cannot find why one month is chosen over another for most of these causes. However, I do find how the month of April came to be designated as national child abuse prevention month:

It was proclaimed National Child Abuse Prevention Month in 1983. The designation was created by the Administration of Children and Families under the U.S. Department of Health and Human Services, and was originally created to ensure the welfare of children. In the 1980's Congress recognized the alarming rate at which children continued to be abused and so proclaimed April the first National Child Abuse Prevention Month as a way to heighten awareness. Since then, child abuse and neglect awareness activities have been promoted across the country during April each year. Has it helped anyone I wonder?

Clicking once again from one website to another, my fingers getting tired now, I am suddenly blind-sided by these facts on www.childhelp.org:

Every ten seconds of every day, there is a report of child abuse.

Every day, up to five children die as a result of child abuse.

90% of child sex abuse victims know the perpetrator in some way.

I look down at Maggie, one of my golden retrievers, curled at my feet and am brought back to thoughts of Bradley. He not only sexually abused little girls, but almost killed five of them. I read the sentence again. *Every ten seconds of every day there is a report….* and yet only two people in fourteen years reported Bradley?

Why? How could this be?

Evidence

By now the damp fog has lifted, giving way to sunshine. I am writing from my library where I can hear the TV in my bedroom and am suddenly aware of those mismatched tones indicating that whatever TV Show was on had been broken into for important news. The OPRAH Show is on air and this particular show is about child molestation – it is still the month of Child Abuse Prevention. *Breaking news on the Bradley case,* I hear and immediately race to the bedroom to learn what is going on.

Attorney General Beau Biden and lead prosecutor Paula Ryan stand before reporters during a press conference to announce new charges against Dr. Earl Bradley. It is jaw-dropping news. New charges? This news envelopes me as the fog had earlier this morning.

On the TV, our Attorney General is saying that a grand jury has indicted Bradley on *58 new charges involving 24 additional victims, all girls.* The evidence for the new charges was gathered from 14 hours of video seized from Bradley's home and office in back in December 2009. This new indictment will proceed as a separate case from the trial that is now slated for February 2011.

The felony charges now stand at 529 counts against 103 children.

Seated on the bench in front of my bed, ram rod straight, intent on the news, I think back to that night I sat in this same position, in front of his home on Savannah Road in downtown Lewes. One stark light illuminated a tiny room toward the back of the house causing shadows against the grayish-white walls. I sat in my car in front of his home several times in the darker evenings of winter and watched. Just watched what was usually a dark, quiet home with a little sign on the front door that read "no trespassing" – it would later be changed to "Beware of Dog." Everything about the house seemed secretive. Now I wonder: Could they have found this evidence on that night where I'd seen the light on in the back of his house?

Even though I watch this press conference through the lens of a TV camera, I can sense the local media frenzy as reporters crush forward to get closer to the podium with their microphones and cameras.

"These charges are the next step forward in our continued efforts to hold Bradley accountable for his actions," The AG says at the Delaware Department of Justice Office in Georgetown.

The new indictment against Earl Bradley now stands at 529 counts of rape, unlawful sexual contact, continuous sexual abuse of a child and sexual exploitation, involving patients of Bradley's from 1999 to 2009. His bail has been raised to $5.29 million cash. Biden then says "If convicted of all charges, Bradley faces life in prison."

The latest news on the case renders me speechless. The number 471 flabbergasted me. Now, it feels as though my heart is slowing down; trying to hoard oxygen as it slams against my chest in seemingly slow motion beats. 529 counts....I close my eyes and think *take slow deep breaths, deep breaths.*

Fury

I'm in my library searching the blogs on the Bradley case, and they are blazing: "Oh just save us from all this crap and hang him. What ever happened to public hangings anyway?"

"Dr. Bradley, guess what? There's a prison shank with your name on it."

"We need a genocide for pedophiles." Although not written properly, I get her point: Round up all the pedophiles, gas them, torture them, systematically exterminate them as had occurred during the Holocaust.

So much anger. And from others, the proverbial, typical question: "Where were the parents?"

I am afraid to get involved in these blogs or they too will consume my life. But I feel a desperate urge, at the very least, to defend the parents. This question about the parents with its implied judgment, still angers me more than all the others. It continues to be the only question where I find myself getting overly defensive.

Later at the local coffee shop, Gail who works there, asks "Have you seen the latest?" She points to the *News Journal*.

I grab the last copy which always sells out when Bradley is on the front page. Today the headline shouts, "Bradley's Sister Sounded Alarm."

Gail says, "So many people didn't listen to the voices in their head."

"I know."

"I think someone had to know something."

"Maybe. But there was no proof back then."

"Proof? Who cares – there was plenty of suspicion."

"But the cops need probable cause to arrest and they didn't have it," I say.

"And they probably second-guessed themselves when questioning the authority of a *doctor*," Gail says. "But what I really want to know is what were those parents *thinking* to leave their child alone?"

I feel the hairs on my neck sizzle – my ears burn with the anger I know is about to burst and that I don't want to get into this with Gail.

"OK – pretend *I* was their doctor" I say. "You know me. You trust me. Why would you even *think* to suspect me?"

"What do you mean? It doesn't matter who the doctor is. You never leave your kids alone. With anyone!"

"I just mean, you wouldn't think to question me if you <u>really</u> trusted me," I say to her.

"It doesn't matter." She is becoming angry with frustration almost snarling at me.

"Gail, hindsight is 20/20. This was a guy who spent years grooming his patients to believe in him, to like him. He was a sociopath – no guilt, no remorse, nothing." I find my voice becoming louder now and try to deflect the anger by flipping a couple of pages of the paper. My foot taps as she begins to make my coffee. "Sometimes he didn't even take them out of the room," I continue, "and if he did he was back in less than four minutes. And sometimes if the mother was in the room, he'd put himself between the parent and child, obscuring the parents' view, and shove his hand right up the diaper."

As the steamy milk is poured for my latte, she looks up. "I didn't realize some of the parents were right there, I –"

"He had a tiny camera hidden in a friggin' pen for God's sake. He fooled everyone."

"A camera in a pen? While the parents were in the same room? I – I didn't know -" Gail slips my coffee into the cup sleeve and gently hands it to me.

"You got it Gail. He fooled everyone."

Missed Opportunities

Bradley, in 1994, then a married father of four, left Pennsylvania on the heels of a police investigation. There were claims by a mother that she heard her 21-month year old daughter scream and found the doctor in a darkened room with her, his hand down her diaper. Bradley accused the mother of trying to extort money from him and authorities cleared him of wrongdoing. Bradley then moved to Delaware, was licensed here in April of 1994, but by law the Delaware Board of Medical Practice was supposed to conduct its own inquiry.

Supposed to…

This is the first in a series of missed opportunities to stop him.

In that same year, 1994, Beebe medical center, our small but well-respected community hospital hired Bradley. In his first two years with the hospital he became known as a brilliant diagnostician, saving the lives of children. A friend told me how Bradley saved her brother's life sometime around the year 2000. Apparently at age seven the young boy began to display life-threatening symptoms, saw five different specialists and no one could find the problem. Bradley solved the puzzle, diagnosing heart trouble. Even so, two years later other medical professionals began to question Bradley's clinical practices.

I take another sip of my morning coffee and look up from the papers spread all over the counter top now. I gaze outside through my sunroom into the deepening green of the landscape and think about how so many of the details of this story seem ironic, even paradoxical: A doctor pedophile who saves lives; a doctor pedophile with a foundation to save babies lives; exam rooms decorated in Disney; doctor….pedophile.

In 1996 while Bradley practiced at Beebe Medical Center, a nurse complained about his excessive catheterizations of girls and how he positioned older patients on their hands and knees while examining labial adhesions. She said Bradley put numbing cream on girls so they wouldn't feel anything. She also expressed concern that Bradley made girls undress before routine exams, kissed and hugged them, and made suggestive remarks about patients' mothers. His 'unusual' method of catheterizations stopped soon after Beebe Hospital launched its own investigation.

Beebe Hospital's investigation concluded that Bradley's use of catheters was "within the mainstream of current pediatric practices." The CEO of the hospital said he considered the complaint "clinical," not sexual.

The hospital claims that no records exist regarding Bradley. Later, they will claim that no records existed regarding complaints. But the hospital *had* looked into the nurses' complaint and concluded his catheterization practice was "within the mainstream of pediatric practices." Nonetheless, it is during this timeframe in 1997 when the hospital decided to assign a chaperone to work with Bradley. In response Bradley threatened to sue the hospital for 'damaging his reputation.' Beebe did an about-face and paid Bradley $10,000 to settle his threat to sue. Meanwhile, while the doctor built his own private practice, Beebe continued to grant him privileges to treat patients and attend to births at the hospital.

I am fuming now. They actually *paid* him $10,000 to go away; to not sue the hospital.

I quickly turn the thin newspaper page almost ripping it when I read that Bradley's peers at the hospital elected him Chief of Pediatrics from September 1998 to June 2002. Again, I am stunned to read this knowing what we now know about Bradley.

Another ridiculous irony.

Not until 2004 when a parent at his satellite office in Milford, Delaware, twenty miles north of Lewes, told local police her daughter complained that "he gave her too many kisses," did Bradley come to the attention of the local police.

Milford

Milford is the kind of town where families go to church on Sunday. And if they don't, they are likely to be asked about it on Monday morning.

Milford: Mostly a farming town. So much so that back in the early 1900s, farmers didn't sell their silos or barns or land – the town just grew up around, and in between, them. It's also a town of blue collar workers, middle class neighbors and farmers all rolled into one quaint, little area. Like 'Mayberry,' Milford appears to be a time capsule of sorts: Grey-stoned, slate-roofed, leaded-window churches dot each curvy street – and on Front Street you'll find an authentic, century-old *Downtowne Barber Shop* complete with spinning red and blue barber pole and the original thick-leathered, metal barber chairs. The center of town converges at Front and Walnut Street with the proverbial funeral parlor and the Milford Chronicle across the street from antique stores and the Dolce café. Old and new, modern and traditional, meld together in this tinier than tiny slice of history.

The melodic bells of the church on Front Street begin to toll and they are lovely; it seems so easy here, so harmonious. Like being transported to another time, another place. This is where Dr. Earl Bradley first began to practice 'pediatrics' in 1994; a place where no one would suspect the likes of a baby molester living in their midst.

The sun paints the sky deep red as day turns to night. Tomorrow would turn hot and humid with scattered showers expected – another day reading, writing and obsessing about the sociopath doctor down the street.

More Complaints

I am again at my kitchen counter, staring at newspaper articles about Bradley. I return to the page detailing the story of the 2004 Police interview when police questioned medical personnel at his office following a mother's complaint that he kissed her child too much. I learn that other colleagues including pediatrician Lowell Scott Jr., said he sometimes referred to Bradley as a "pedophile." Scott later told a news reporter that his remark was taken 'out of context.'

One 7-year-old's grandmother said he pulled down the girl's underwear and violated her with his hand during an exam in 2003.

Another mother said her 3-year-old said Bradley "kissed her tongue" when he took her to a room alone.

In 2005, Milford police wanted to charge Bradley with offensive touching. Prosecutors decided they did not have enough evidence. Still, no one reported Bradley to the medical disciplinary board. No one. Even though state law requires medical professionals and police to report any physician they believe to be guilty of unprofessional conduct.

I read and re-read the details about Bradley's half-sister who worked at his practice, *Baybees*, as his office manager. In late 2004 the trade association for physicians, the Medical Society of Delaware, received a complaint from her about Bradley. Another mistake in a long line of blunders because the Medical *Board* is responsible for disciplining (or helping) doctors in trouble. The Medical *Society* is not. Barnes told police that Bradley took antidepressants from patient samples and was deep in debt. She also said that parents often complained that he touched their children inappropriately. She put her concerns in writing to the Medical <u>Society</u> of Delaware.

No one reported Bradley to the State Medical <u>Board</u>.

I wonder what could have driven his own sister to this point – the point where she could turn on the brother who employed her. I heard that he had also verbally and physically abused her. I suppose after all she'd heard, seen and experienced herself, she'd had enough and tried to do what was right. She apparently faxed a letter to the Society detailing her complaints but the copy given to investigators did not include the part about inappropriate touching.

Society officials blamed this omission of this paragraph on a malfunctioning fax machine.

I think a fax machine? One silly little blip by an old-fashioned piece of technology and they never knew.

Never knew. The part. About touching little girls. Had someone only taken that extra step, asked questions about the missing words or speckled spaces on that second page, perhaps this, in combination with what the hospital knew, could have helped police put the pieces of the Bradley puzzle together sooner.

But then someone, supposedly, did. Try. Barnes said Dr. James P. Marvel Jr., then the society's president and a friend of Bradley's at Beebe Hospital, told Barnes he took the issue seriously. I read that Marvel made an appointment with Bradley to discuss the allegations by his sister. But he didn't have all the facts because page 2 of Barnes' faxed letter got stuck on top of page one. He didn't see the allegations of Bradley inappropriately touching children. No wonder Marvel deemed Barnes' complaints a "family matter." He commented how Bradley was held in high regard at Beebe. Then too, so was Dr. Marvel. He is the great grandson of the hospital's founder; one of the original Beebe Brothers.

It's a small town and history goes a long way here.

I've accomplished no real work here today. As usual, it has been usurped by Earl Bradley. But I begin to wonder about Dr. Marvel again. Am I just being naïve? Did he know more was going on with Bradley and chose not to take action, instead burying his head like others before him had done? No, I think. It couldn't be. *No one <u>knowingly</u> hides a pedophile.* Or, maybe, because he didn't know all the facts and because this was a highly respected doctor of the family that is Beebe, he chose to believe what he wanted. What bothers me is that I know Bradley worked at Beebe at the same time as Marvel. I know they were colleagues and I know they were friendly during the time a chaperone had been assigned to work with Bradley.

How could Marvel *not* have put two and two together and come up with the fact that it was more than *just* a family matter? As I write this, Marvel is one of three doctors being sued in civil court along with Beebe Medical Center.

The Case Escalates

By 2008 several more parents told police about inappropriate vaginal exams and touching.

A 12-year-old girl who saw Bradley at his practice for pink eye said he gave her a vaginal exam and penetrated her with his fingers.

A 6-year-old seeking evaluation for possible attention deficit disorder was given a physical and Bradley touched her genital area. Afterward Bradley kissed her several times and asked if she wanted to stay overnight with him.

An 8-year old looking for treatment for excessive urination was given three vaginal exams over a period of weeks. Bradley did not wear gloves, kissed her on the lips and took her to the *prize* room. It was in the prize room, on the grey couch, that Bradley sexually abused over one hundred babies and young children – all girls, one boy.

Toward the end of 2008, detectives prepared another search warrant for Bradley's office. One year prior to the final arrest. One full year. How many children would be seen in his office in that time period? How many sexually assaulted? A Sussex county judge denied that application for the search warrant but told a state trooper "they could arrest the doctor because he would sign a criminal arrest warrant." Although reporters and investigators have tried, no one knows *who* that judge was or why he wouldn't sign a search warrant. The investigation into suspicions about Bradley didn't move forward for another year because there was no hard evidence to arrest him.

Another missed chance.

Still, the state prosecutor's office was building their case during this time frame, late 2008 to the fall of '09. They watched Bradley. They would continue to do so until the hard evidence to stop him materialized in the fall of 2009 when he would finally be stopped.

How could it have taken so long?

Bradley's 'aura' as a respected physician helped him escape prosecution. Patients, who included many lower-income immigrants and Medicaid recipients, might have been intimidated. There was an imbalance of power that made it unlikely for parents to protest.

And who could dream this could happen to the level it did, here, in the place it did?

Who could imagine?

Here, in a place where soaring snow geese blissfully glide over our lakes and land.

Here in this town with its Victorian homes and wide porches.

Here, where dolphin fins break through cresting waves and children build giant sandcastles.

The Last Year

Bradley's attacks on children are among "the most violent and brutal on a child of any age" said the lead computer forensic detective. In one, Bradley cruelly tells a crying child he is abusing to "smile for the cameras." In another, a girl screams and attempts to run away before he captures her and then forces her to engage in intercourse.

In that last year alone before his arrest – there are red flags, warning signs, missed opportunities. It is reported that forty-seven 'new' children were raped or abused during that time period. I repeat the number forty-seven in my head and can almost picture the red flags. They flutter in the wind just as the wings of the snow geese do, each and every winter.

Throughout 2009 as police and special investigators watched Bradley, they waited for key evidence that would allow them to search Bradley's property and make an arrest stick.

In December of 2009 the case, finally, breaks open with the Jane Doe #1 (I will call her Melissa) evidence.

Earl Bradley is then arrested and by early February 2010 the charges would be 529 counts of abuse against more than 103 children. In an arrest affidavit, police said they observed recordings of Bradley forcing young girls, even babies, to perform intercourse and oral sex. Sometimes he screamed at crying victims. In the February indictment, prosecutors wrote that five children appeared to stop breathing during Bradley's attacks. Bradley was, until trial, held on $5.29 million bail at Vaughn Correctional Center near Smyrna.

It is dark now. The house is quiet now. Only the sharp light from my computer pulses into the night of this day. Flexing and un-flexing, I type, trying to unravel my angry thoughts.

Secrets

Some secrets take us to the edge. Some secrets cripple lives.

Months after Bradley's arrest, secrets flourished. Many had known or heard the rumors about Bradley. A handful of nurses and doctors as well as parents who were lucky enough to have heard talk about Bradley's 'odd' behavior and were saved from taking their child to his practice. But there were also those who thought something 'just wasn't right' with Bradley but ignored this feeling.

If only they'd made their fears known.

But they didn't.

Most did nothing.

Nothing. This word reverberates in my head as I wait in line at Starbucks practically across the street from Bradley's old place. I am so lost in thought that I hear Pam as if from far away saying, "Hi Meg. The usual?" I blink, stare and come unto myself again saying, "Oh, Hi Pam. Sorry, lost in thought. Yes, a Meg Special."

After returning to my car, I sit for a while. I turn the heat on – it's still chilly in the early days of Spring. There are still traces of the blizzards of 2010; the mountains of snow melt; the brilliant white turns gray and black. Those storms.

I still cannot get over the fact that, in parking lots, snow had been piled as high as two-story buildings.

I still cannot get over the heavy, blinding whiteness of it all.

I still cannot believe these storms so soon after Bradley's crimes, how both have crippled life here at the beach.

I think about the people that didn't do more. Those who knew or suspected and were...what? Afraid? Perhaps these people thought, "Stay on your own path, it's not my concern." But is this any different from a crime committed in Toledo, Ohio when a 26 year old woman was raped in broad daylight as she walked from her friend's house to the library? The neighborhood was one of densely packed homes. No one stopped to help; motorists kept driving by. She asked a pedestrian after the assailant fled if she could use his cell phone to call for help. He kept walking. Why? So many saw it, yet didn't try to stop it, didn't try to help. Or the woman who screamed for help from her 5th story window in New York city as someone tried to stab her. No one bothered. In both these and Bradley's case, was it "turning a blind eye" out of fear? In the Bradley case, is it the possibility of shame in that 'what if I accuse a doctor and I am wrong?"

They may have all had different reasons for not helping to stop these crimes but in each case, the perpetrator won. A woman is raped, another, murdered.

Multiple children are abused.

Not Guilty

In the local news broadcast tonight, March 24: "Earl Bradley accused of raping patients was back in court briefly today – entering a plea of NOT GUILTY, he faces 471 charges with more than 100 alleged victims."

Several parents were in court today, some in tears, some who wanted to see their former doctor, one they say they once trusted. Only the media presence rivaled the security on hand this day as former pediatrician Earl Bradley arrived at the Sussex County Courthouse. One parent said on

Meg Ellacott

camera, "He doesn't look like the same doctor I once knew. Someone who was a friend. We never dreamed he could do something like this." She wiped her runny nose. Escorted by a half-dozen security guards, Bradley left the courthouse wearing the Department of Corrections' gray jumpsuit as well as his Disney World denim jacket. The arraignment lasted only a few moments. His hands and ankles handcuffed, he walked slowly through the courthouse just as he did during his arraignment. He appeared emotionless, looking at the ground. He'd lost weight from his original 220 pound frame.

As quickly as his court appearance started, Bradley was whisked away in a white van with a blue car trailing. With tires screeching they race away from the courthouse through the tight streets of Georgetown. I watch the news on my flat screen TV wishing I was there in person. But because this was the first in a series of trials and hearings, I wasn't sure if the public, media, those not involved in the case are allowed to attend. I learn, albeit late, they are and plan to attend all in the future. "Bradley heads back to prison until his next day in court even though his trial, in the minds of most parents, has already ended." One of the broadcasters briefly summarizes Bradley's crimes and gets reactions to the plea of NOT GUILTY. One parent's response: "We expected something different. We weren't just surprised, we were stunned. We still can't believe it happened." I too am stunned Bradley pleads not guilty when the videotapes show otherwise. "How can this be?" I ask.

67

Fooled

At last, it is April. I await relief from one of the harshest winters on record. As for the doctors and medical personnel who trusted Bradley, more news hits the street with a four-page article in The News Journal. Is it my imagination or are the headlines on Bradley getting bigger, more bold and blacker with every report? This one screams "Hospital Heard Allegations about Bradley 14 Years Ago." The tag line says "Facing 18 lawsuits in case, Beebe could go into bankruptcy."

"After four months of revealing little of what they knew about pediatrician Earl B. Bradley, administrators at Beebe Medical Center now say they investigated a 1996 report that he inappropriately touched young girls." So, they're coming clean, I think. Perched upon the kitchen stool with the paper spread out before me, I think Well, they have to – don't they? I wonder about the possibility of bankruptcy for our only hospital. I'd worried when the number of suits was just four, but eighteen!

Many months later, the number of suits against the hospital and four doctors would grow to thirty-three. One day, over eight months from the time I write this, who could guess that those 18 and then 33 would turn into 88 against our small local hospital. Years later, the 88 will turn into a class action suit. "Hospital officials say they fear the suits could force the hospital into bankruptcy. This is an astonishing and heartbreaking, reversal of fortune for a hospital founded nearly a century ago, one that treats tens of thousands of patients each year both here and in satellite offices," said one report in the paper.

I Google Beebe and find it hires 1300 employees and earns $238 million in annual revenues. For a small hospital, Beebe has grown strong and formidable. After struggling for years with a reputation for relatively poor medical service, they have finally evolved into a top-rated community hospital. I know they are ranked in the top 5% in the nation by a website called Healthgrades. I learn they won the Distinguished Hospital Award for Clinical Excellence and I know Beebe now has an award winning orthopedics department as well as awards in coronary intervention.

I think of all the skilled doctors, administrators and other medical personnel the hospital has brought here to live and work. It is not easy to lure talented doctors to this rural area where the pay scales are lower, where Medicare and Medicaid pays less than in larger, more densely populated cities.

Now the nonprofit hospital stands accused in court of dereliction of duty and medical negligence.

"Oh God," I say out loud. These words sound so criminal, so abhorrent and I find that I feel sorry for the hospital even as I simultaneously sympathize with the parents – the children. I feel that acidic bubble in the pit of my stomach again.

The suits contend the hospital could have prevented attacks by Bradley if the staff had reported him in 2005 to Delaware's Board of Medical Practice, which licenses and disciplines physicians.

The article goes on to say how the disclosures are a turnabout from the hospital's posture just days after Bradley's December 16 arrest when officials at Beebe said they had 'no inkling of any past problems with Bradley.' Again I think, Oh God. How will they ever recover from the lies?

Dazed

A few days later in the same month of April I read: "The acts perpetrated by Bradley on his young victims and their families did not spare Beebe Medical Center. A number of our own employees have identified their children as victims." This statement has me feeling more sad than I did before. Even their own employees; those who are part of the hospital family. At the same time, I'm feeling somewhat manipulated. Of course, I feel sorry for the Beebe parents, but why are they any different than all the other families? If the hospital had been more cautious, more vigilant, more watchful five years ago when concerns about Bradley were raised, again and again, maybe he could have been stopped sooner. I'm feeling confused, almost dazed by it all.

There are just so many mind-boggling details. Still, in the end, what I believe is simply this: no one *knowingly* hides a pedophile. Beebe could have done a better job five years ago, so could his sister, so could law enforcement, so could the judge who didn't dispense the search warrant, so could the then state's Attorney General (Jane Brady) and so could medical personnel within Bradley's office. In the end, balls were dropped, miscommunication abounded and no one followed through. But I simply cannot, will not, believe that any one knew the extent to which Bradley had gone.

Among all the news articles on Bradley, a small editorial appears, one I'd thought of myself. At its conclusion a woman named Catherine Rose says, "Rather than being known as the community where that awful pedophile doctor lived, why not be known as the community that gave an all-out effort to say: No more abusing our children."

Clues

It's the oldest human choice: comfortable ignorance or knowledge bought with pain. At his trial for heresy it was Socrates who said "For man, an unexamined life is not worth living." But how could the parents of Bradley's victims have known? Who could bring themselves to consider that their a doctor could do this to their children? I know they asked themselves, "Why didn't I see the warning signs?"

I too ask "How could *I* have ever predicted when I started writing about this, that it would come to this?" Or that I too would feel their pain so deeply.

Internal Investigations

George Bernard Shaw said "the single biggest problem with communication is the illusion that it has taken place."

So many red flags, so many clues. No one stopped him; no one turned him in. Some tried and did not succeed. The internal investigations by Beebe Medical Center and the State of Delaware are complete now. The results announced in endless newspaper articles and played out in the drama that is television and sidewalk chatter.

"A mass tragedy of this magnitude could have been pre-empted if the individuals directly involved had been alert, less willing to give Bradley the benefit of the doubt, and if they had scrupulously followed the law. Systems were in place to catch a perpetrator, but, they were either not properly assessed, or when called upon, human and mechanical error prevented the appropriate actions from being taken," said Linda L. Ammons of Widener University Law School. Delaware Governor Jack Markell tapped Ammons to undertake an independent review of 'who knew what when' and the state's handling of complaints, regarding accused pedophile pediatrician Dr. Earl B. Bradley. She delivered her findings on May 11, 2010. It was over seventy pages long.

After four months of talking to almost sixty people locally, around the country and doing this work pro bono in an exhaustive examination of the facts and circumstances, Ammons called the criminal case against Bradley on charges of rape and molestation "perhaps the worst pedophilia case of the century." She wrote that no one mandated by Delaware law to report child abuse had forwarded information about Bradley to state agencies in the manner required by current law. No one. Only two people – Lt. Kenneth Brown of the Milford Police Department and Lynda Barnes, Bradley's sister and former office manager, had attempted to call attention to suspicions about Bradley's behavior.

Because no one listened to the voices in their head or perhaps chose instead to ignore them, the pediatrician was able to continue practicing despite complaints about his behavior first raised in Pennsylvania in 1994. She also noted in her summary: That through a combination of Bradley's cunning, carelessness and inattention by the Medical Society of Delaware and Beebe Medical Center, communication breakdowns and lack of action by a medical board with a reputation for protecting the very individuals it is meant to police, Bradley was never stopped.

His Youth

Springtime and another report appears in the news about those who knew Bradley. One segment in particular sparks a question in me and I ask: Had abuse at the hands of Bradley's own father changed the course of Bradley's life, casting a shadow over a future that once held so much promise? Or maybe it was Earl Bradley's uncle who had somehow altered his life's course.

It is reported that Bradley's uncle, Dr. William Bradley (with his master's degree in clinical psychology and doctorate in education) was accused of a series of misdemeanor charges of various deviate sexual behaviors. After a bench trial in the Centre County Court of Common Pleas in Pennsylvania, William Bradley was convicted of indecent exposure, two counts of indecent assault and open lewdness, but was found not guilty of involuntary deviate sexual behavior. Court documents indicate that William had exposed himself to three minor girls, but the most serious charge involved a 4 year old girl that the elder Bradley had approached and lured into his back yard. He not only exposed himself, but asked her to perform oral sex. Testifying in his own defense, William Bradley denied the charges, claiming the testimony by the 4-year-old had been coached.

It is June. Spring continues to unfold. Usually warmer by now, it is a chilly day when I return home to write. Grabbing the remote, I pop on the gas fireplace and stare into the flickering flames, my back and shoulders warmed by the heat of the fire.

I learned recently that Bradley's mother was a notorious alcoholic and that he lost both his mother and father by age fourteen. I can't help but think how other things in his younger life must have been hurtful or shameful: A father who reportedly read child porn, an uncle who was arrested for sexually molesting a child, even this, a mother who was known in their town as a drunk. I can't help but think too that Bradley must have been exposed to, and abused by, either his father or uncle. He was just too sick *not* to have been. Statistics show that most pedophiles experience some form of sexual abuse as a child.

This knowledge prompts me to want to understand more about Bradley's earlier years. What could have made him like that? I am about to do some of my own investigating when an article appears in the *News Journal*. Beginning as most Bradley articles do, on the front page. I bring it to my kitchen counter top, smooth out the thin pages and hungrily read on for more clues.

'Nobody is Born Like That' the headline reads while the sub-title printed in smaller letters beneath, reads *Jailed Doctor has Past Marked by Family Chaos, Death, Solitude.* Below the paper's header is a picture of Bradley on the day of his arrest in his Mickey Mouse jacket.

That jacket.

The irony of this photo, I'm sure, will haunt me as long as I write this story. Perhaps for long afterward.

Disney. A pedophile pediatrician. A most disturbing image of a man who made up a pretend world using Disney characters to lure children.

How dare he, I think, each time I see him in that jacket. He'd been arrested in it and the media had shown that same video clip again and again.

The unmitigated gall. One more sick twist that he'd pretend to love everything Disney and then turn around and molest the children who adored Disney as well.

Another photo in this article depicts a younger Earl Bradley during his days at Temple University. One in which he appears angry, glaring at the lens of the camera. Another photo depicts an even younger Bradley that already hints of a sad, fearful young man. I don't really know why I say this except for his sorrowful eyes. There is no youthful joy in them; they are like the eyes of an old man; despondent.

As I study the photos, I wonder why he appears this way. So lost. Is it just my imagination projecting this fearfulness on to Bradley as a young man because I figure, he just had to be?

How *had* he been violated as a child? I know he'd been abandoned. How *had* he been emotionally traumatized? Is it only in *my* mind where I see such a troubled young man? Because I want, no - need – to have a reason? Again and again I am compelled to know why and how he could have done this.

The paper says, Bradley appeared to have led a life that was ghostlike in both pre-med and medical school. "A loner;

moody and like most sociopaths, brooding; he directs his energy inward; he is remote; guarded." One classmate who was interviewed didn't even realize Bradley had been in several classes with him until the newspaper contacted him.

The portrait of who Bradley was and why he was this way, starts to take shape as I read on: The alcoholic mother, the one protective sister, the abusive and sexually deviant father, the loneliness, the isolation, the oddness, the childhood chaos, the escalation of his sicknesses.

But before all the degrees, before becoming a doctor, before all the patients, he was just a little boy, a sullen, sometimes depressed one, but from all accounts, normal still. Normal.

He was a son, a nephew, a brother. He became a husband and a father.

One of the first hints that something was off with Earl Bradley was in his twenty's. While enrolled in Temple University's School of Medicine, Bradley applied for a seat on the schools' admission board, a highly respected and coveted position. The young med student, usually brooding and quiet, revealed his darker side when promoting his candidacy in an essay. His *formal* letter was written in crayon and magic marker. It railed against the whole admissions system, saying "it took him seven times to get accepted." I am not shocked. Just a little surprised to read such a specific clue into the student's strange behavior; another glimpse into Bradley's paranoia and rage. It seems crazy to me that he would have been permitted to remain on the admissions board or in any more important role for that matter. Didn't anyone react to this bizarre behavior? *This bizarre behavior*. It is the same question I ask when he worked for Beebe Medical Center some thirty years later, when again no one there seemed to react either.

Reading on I learn that after Bradley finished his pediatrics residency in 1986, he worked on the staff of Frankford Hospital in Pennsylvania. As it is for most medical residents, these must have been tough years, long hours, difficult patients, but it was also a time when he'd meet his future wife. And the time when the rumors and whispers about him would begin.

I learn that Bradley's half-sister, Linda Barnes, said her brother's early childhood was chaotic. She told the Medical Society, "that his parents were extremely dysfunctional." Again I wonder about the roles they played and how their 'dysfunction' shaped Bradley's earlier years.

There is a photo of him in this article in his late teens, early twenty's. He wears a beard and has thick shaggy hair. He is squinting, peering through thick lens. Words and sentences like odd, awkward, demons – *what could have compelled him - recorded videos of the attacks* – swirl through my brain.

There are other slices of information from his younger years: How Earl had trouble connecting with peers as a youth and later with adults; his unusual fascination with toys – his messy hair and dirty clothes; a filthy, dirty home. One psychiatrist states "that he had risk factors for severe personality pathology even as young adult." I think of how his mother died of a sudden subdural hemorrhage and how *at* her funeral, his father suffered a heart attack and died;

how this broad-shouldered young man scowled, squinted, glowered at the camera.

Moving from the big city of Philadelphia to the small town of Milford Delaware probably wasn't that easy. But maybe he thought it would allow him to become the 'country doctor' he'd seen depicted in those Norman Rockwell paintings.

Life-Changes

After some years in Milford he moved to Lewes and took a job at Beebe Medical Center. This was in 1994, and was another stepping stone to the goal of owning his own practice. But at Beebe, the whispers got louder. Suspicions heightened.

Even so, he was made Chief of Pediatrics in 1998 soon after coming to Beebe Medical. The years prior to '98 were a time when the economy was good. A time when Bradley's four children, in their teens, flourished. They were good times and it seemed as though everything Bradley touched turned profitable. Most of his investments were in real estate and land with stocks and municipal funds held under Bradley's limited liability corporation – Bradley Family LLC.

This changed in 1998.

His wife, Susanne was a young professional with both nursing and law degrees; a mother of four. She'd divorce Bradley in 1998. How could she have left him with four children still in their teens, I'd ask. Four children that must have needed guidance.

What did she know?

What didn't she know?

The children stayed. She left. Did she just walk out one day? No one knows the answers to these questions. She won't speak to anyone; it's as if she never knew him. What happened I'd ask again and again? I learn she moved to the Washington D.C. area but refuses all requests for interviews.

I am devouring every morsel of this long article now. But my confusion, or curiosity, is heightened by thinking again about his wife leaving him. Bound by hate and driven by fear, is this when and where his crimes begin to escalate? I can't help but ask the question others want answered: Did he molest his own children? I don't know the answers to this except what I've heard around town; that his three daughters were 'lovely' polite young women and that his son may have been the only one who suffered neglect and abuse by his father. I learn too that within months after Bradley's arrest, one of his daughters was forced to drop out of college because other students had heard about her father's case and treated her poorly.

It was post-divorce in December 2001 that Bradley purchased the property where he'd one day open the practice: Baybees, 18259 Coastal Hwy, Lewes, Delaware. He purchased it all - the land, the larger house and other shack-like buildings for $240,000 – a good price for prime real estate right off route 1, Coastal Highway and about ten minutes to the beaches of Rehoboth or Lewes.

Although Bradley's investments once appeared lucrative, he soon became as erratic in his bill paying, bill collections and upkeep as he was in the poor administration of Baybees

Pediatrics. At the time of his arrest he owed back taxes on the land and property. His home, too, while a good initial purchase, had fallen into a state of disrepair. Many things in Bradley's life seemed to have fallen into *states of disrepair*..

And so I have my clues as to some of the catalysts that twisted Earl Bradley's mind. I am sad, exhausted, all at once. A feeling of emptiness washes through me and I haven't a clue why. Is it because none of the pieces feel like they are coming together or making sense? Could this be what is causing such angst? I begin to feel there are no answers. Maybe there just isn't any sense to the violence or pain he inflicted. Maybe it. Maybe he. Simply, is.

What I do know is that Bradley grew into a man with extreme depression, grave insecurities, debilitating shyness, immense fear, anger and hatred. Paradoxically, Bradley ends as he began, isolated and alone.

Predators

The rain outside sounds heavy. The warm weather is here as the giant iris and blue bells take bloom. I can tell, even through the tightly closed wooden blinds, that it is dark outside. I slide open the blinds to see deep gray storm clouds move swiftly across the sky. It is the kind of sky that warns of an approaching storm. I expect thunder but it never comes.

I move to the kitchen and slip onto a kitchen stool settling in to re-read on my laptop the article on the hospital's investigation. The light over the kitchen island is good for reading. Before I can find the article though, a new headline pops up: "Hospital Heard Allegations about

Bradley 14 Years ago" and again I feel the wind whoosh from my lungs. They knew the allegations. They *knew*.

I think about how many ordinary, everyday things occur in a fourteen year time span. How many couples meet, marriages are made, lovers break up, kids are born – and how it can all happen in a quarter of a lifetime. Over 5000 midnights. Over 5000 sunsets. All those children. My stomach lurches. 5000 ordinary days and nights. The hospital, other doctors. Parents. All their suspicions…their actions, their in-actions. Nothing stopped the predator.

Other Cases

By this time, a half of a year since his arrest, I'd read nearly a hundred articles and blog pages. Articles like A Day in the Life of Earl Bradley Behind Bars; Former Lewes pediatrician's License suspended; Pedophile Doctors not New, Not Rare; Mind of a Predator. The articles are chronologically ordered now in their new blue file folders. I learn of the cases seemingly every day now or perhaps I am more attuned to them since Bradley usurped this part of my life. These stories seem to appear on any given day, in any given TV show, magazine or serious discussion. The numerous stories and cases of predators.

In California authorities tried for years to bring charges against a child psychiatrist but were thwarted by statutes of limitation until his arrest in April 2007. A jury could not reach a verdict in 2009 on charges that he molested seven boys. He currently awaits his second trial.

In Alabama Dr. Michael Roy Sharpe was charged in 2009 with raping a teenage girl. The doctor had left two

Tennessee hospitals after abuse complaints but was never disciplined by the state's medical board.

In a small town in Cincinnati, twin brother Pediatricians, Mark and Scott Blankenburg befriended teenage boys by sponsoring Little League teams and supplying their victims with cash, drugs and alcohol. Both doctors were sentenced to long prison terms in early 2010.

Another article titled *A Family of Monsters* and *Shattered Faith* about a 62 year old man coming forward to tell about his traumatic molestation at the hands of a catholic priest. These too are stacked in piles on my desk. Some I haven't had the chance to read yet.

Violate

While still reading about Beebe having had suspicions all those years ago, I scan the pages and subheads... "A lot of balls dropped, Beebe records subpoenaed, Beebe staff praised Bradley, Fooled... Trusted... Believed." My eyes widen in an attempt to pull the words in faster. "Too many kisses, strange guy, witnessed, violate her, bipolar, had his hand under their clothing

and – "

The word *violate* sinks within me. My lungs, my throat feels heavy.

Violate. Two pages later that word comes back to me and I feel sick; a thick knot of something climbs to the back of my throat.

After finishing the article I move back to my desk. But a few minutes later, as the clicking of the mouse slows, I take my hands off the computer and calmly place them in my lap. The word *violate* is still with me. I look to my right, through the six-paned window to the dreary day outside. I peer through the Leland Cypress trees out back and am transported to a time some 43 years ago, to a place and time where I too, had been violated. Almost. But I'd fought back.

Suddenly it occurred to me why Bradley had chosen the youngest, the most vulnerable, the powerless: Not only could they not tell because their words hadn't yet formed, but they were too young, too small, to even attempt to fight back, as I had at age thirteen.

Why hadn't I thought of this earlier? Why had it taken me so long to remember?

Four decades ago at North Hills Country Club on Long Island, Timmy and I would go out to the woods after swim club and practice kissing. The woods were deep and dark. I remember slivers of blinding sunlight creeping through tree-top leaves as Timmy and I lay kissing on overgrown roots and grass. The woods bordered the Club's Olympic sized pool and its lush golf greens. Timmy was my first boyfriend – or, so I thought. He 'taught' me how to French kiss and one time, felt my breast. It was a warm, innocent time, those first sexual experiments; the wonder, the misunderstood guilt, knowing, or *believing* he liked me.

One afternoon as Timmy and I lay kissing, two other boys on the swim team, Frankie and Tommy, jumped from behind a cluster of trees. They chased me and shouted "We're gonna get you – you're gonna' give Tim a blow job whether you like it or not!" They caught up to me and dragged me to the ground, hands groping, reaching for the zipper on my plaid madras shorts, grabbing for my breasts. Their hands seemed to be everywhere.

I had no idea what a 'blow job' was. But I knew by the way they were taunting me that it must be bad. More than the terror I felt, I remember feeling horribly betrayed, and then confused; mostly, I felt a growing sense of fear and remember feeling powerless. These were kids I had swam with, dived with, played Marco Polo with. Daily. Our mothers were close friends. *How could they do this to me?* As they groped and pulled and shouted Y*our gonna screw Timmy*, I still had no idea what they were doing or why.

Instinctually I knew I had to get out of this. *God, think, think* - I said to myself as the four of us scrambled and rolled in the sandy dirt. All I knew was that Timmy was *in* on it – is this what hurt most of all? It was the first time I truly understood what the word betrayal meant.

At that instant, out of the corner of my eye I realized I was almost on top of a sand trap. I grabbed a giant handful of sand and threw it, hard, into Timmy's face. He jerked away from me, jumped up, towered over me and screamed "I'm blind – I can't see." He wrestled with himself now trying to rid his eyes of the sandy spray. The other two stood, their eyes trained on Tim.

I ran. I had to get away. I remember running so hard my legs felt like lead weights were attached. And my heart ached – I didn't know if it was from the race back to the pool or from the hurt or from the fear. I didn't know the word rape back then or the word *violate*.

I'm still peering out my living room windows into this dark gray day as this memory washes through me. I am chilled to the bone thinking back to the confusion and the shame. Knowing now I'd had no reason to feel shame and yet....

What must Bradley's victims have felt without words, without strength – with no way to fight back?

He Came To Sussex

Sussex County, Delaware is 950 square miles and is among some of the fastest growing areas in the United States. Its population grew 38% in the nineteen-ninety's and over 10% more recently. As the rural areas of Lewes and Rehoboth Beach grew, so too did its infrastructure; it's roads, it's utilities services, the housing market and its medical facilities. Beebe Medical Center, located in Lewes, is the principle hospital presence in Sussex and one of the largest employers on the Delmarva peninsula, employing over 1,500.

This medical center is where Earl Bradley decided to apply in his specialty in pediatrics in 1994. Perhaps he wanted to make a change, put down roots, raise his family near the beach and eventually start his own practice.

It didn't happen like that.

Home

I'll never forget the day I moved to Rehoboth.

For three years, I searched for my home away from big city living. Each year, three or four times a year, I'd come to Rehoboth and stay at "The Inn on the corner" as I called it, or its real name, The Homestead. Mary and Judy, the innkeepers, manage this quaint, Bed & Breakfast, where they accept dogs, no kids. So this was the place for me each fall, winter and spring when I'd pile my two golden retrievers, Maggie and Kelly, into the car and head through Annapolis and the Bay Bridge to my search for a new life in Rehoboth. Every time I crossed that bridge, I'd open the windows, smell the fresh salty air, smile to myself and after thirty-five years working my butt off, I'd shout out loud, "Beach Life, here I come!"

I'd looked at more than a hundred homes over the years, never imagining that my dream home was less than ¼ mile from that B&B off Old Landing Road.

Or that a deranged doctor practiced medicine a mile north of Old Landing Road.

Home.

My house, with its one-level living, three bedrooms, soaring cathedral ceilings and fireplace, I was home. With its half-acre of land, snow geese, rabbit and fox foraging for food in the corn fields behind me and its gorgeous landscaping, *I* was home.

While excited, I was sometimes fearful of making this big move by myself. But I grew to know it was the right decision and *finally* it was the right time – time for me to start over at age fifty-six. But it would not be *all* I'd expected. What I'd expected was friendly neighbors, quiet, crime-free streets, everything about the natural beauty that is here, everything about nature itself.

But what I got, was another kind of fear that would slither between my silly life fears and anxieties. Lewes, next door to Rehoboth Beach, was the last place I'd expect to find the kind of crimes committed by anyone, let alone a doctor.

Home.

Beebe

To understand the story of Bradley, I think I must first learn something about Beebe. The story of the Beebe Medical Center dates back almost 100 years to 1916 when two brothers, Drs. James and Richard Beebe, built the Center, the only private hospital in the small state other than the one in Wilmington, two hours away. The brothers dreamed of bringing modern medicine to the rural area of Sussex. Prior to building the four-room hospital in 1916, James and Richard performed emergency operations on a kitchen table in a nearby farmhouse with instruments boiled in water on a kettle stove. In the same year the hospital was founded, Dr. James Beebe distinguished himself in the medical profession by becoming the President of the Medical Society of Delaware; he also helped advance the fight against cancer by dedicating himself to cancer research. His brother, Dr. Richard, served as an army physician overseas and worked to enhance the lives of veterans at home. When WW II struck, Dr. Richard would find the soldiers defending his nation and its allies seeking treatment in the hospital he had helped to found. During the war when a large number of ships were torpedoed off the Atlantic coast, many of the survivors arrived in Lewes in lifeboats and sought treatment at Beebe Hospital.

Today the hospital is still privately owned, one of very few in the nation. It has grown from a 4-bed medical center to a 210-licensed bed, not-for-profit, seaside community hospital. Much of it is paid for by wealthy patrons and businesses such as Joseph Hudson, Benjamin Shaw and Mrs. Henry R. Thompson, John W. Rollins, who have wings named for their generous contributions.

Just as the townspeople are fiercely proud of their town, employees, staff, friends and patrons of Beebe are fiercely protective of this hospital and its historic roots. I'd soon learn this the hard way.

Once I learn that *some* people don't like the fact I am writing this story.

Or that *some* people wish this story would just go away.

But I digress. In 1989 the Beebe Medical Foundation was created with the sole mission to support Beebe Medical Center. $26 million has been raised to fund new programs in community outreach, health fairs and screenings, to purchase new equipment, construct new buildings and expand the current, original building. Because the allegations against Bradley started long before his arrest in 2009, Beebe Medical Center has found itself in the middle of state wide investigations and eventual lawsuits that could cripple the historic hospital.

Tort

Within six months of Bradley's arrest, Beebe Hospital would face 44 civil lawsuits while looking at the possibility of its demise, bankruptcy or sale to a larger hospital management corporation. These disturbing rumors continue to swirl like the rolling tornado spouts that touch down here each summer and fall.

Tort: In civil law, meaning a wrongful act for which damages can be sought by the injured party. Tort: Shortly after the physician's arrest, the civil actions began. Civil actions that included so many, and were so large they would soon transform into a class action suit.

The first civil suit filed against Bradley was submitted by the parents of the child who triggered Bradley's arrest, the child I call "Melissa."

I knew basically what a civil suit was but had to Google its true definition: A type of law suit, brought on by individuals or businesses. If someone owes another person money or any type of 'compensation' and they do not cooperate, than a civil lawsuit can be filed.

The list of civil suits against Bradley began to grow. Lawyers who were handling these 'tort' cases placed ads in the papers, even on television encouraging *any* Bradley patient (ever) to join the class action suit. In these lawsuits, the counts against the hospital spoke to its failure to report sexual abuse perpetrated by Bradley and that defendants had acted in a reckless manner in not doing so.

At first it was only Bradley who was being sued in civil cases brought forth. As more information became available to the public, outraged parents (whether confirmed or not that their child was one of the pediatricians' victims) filed civil suits against both him, three other doctors accused of knowing more but not coming forward, and Beebe Medical Center. One of the lawyers handling one of the civil suits against Beebe said "they" (referring to hospital administrators, staffers and any medical personnel who even suspected) "all had a duty, a legal duty and they did not perform that duty."

How could I have predicted that years later the civil suits would be consolidated into one large class action suit against Beebe Medical Center, five doctors and the Medical Society of Delaware.

Had I been able to search into the future, I would have known that on Saturday, August 4th 2012 *The News Journal* will report that Beebe, accused of dereliction of duty in failing to report the doctor's atrocities, would reach a massive monetary settlement brought by his former patients.

By the end of 2012 the class action would settle for 123 million dollars.

The settlement would be paid by the hospital's insurance company and $6 million in cash from the hospital itself and $1 million in hospital services for the victims. Other funds came from insurance carriers for the doctors also named in the suit and the Medical Society of Delaware would pay.

Although the original case proves that over 100 children were molested on tape, *anyone* who was a patient of Bradley's, whether their child was a victim or not, was permitted to join the class action suit. Well over one thousand families did – a great deal more than the legal firms handling the case, anticipated.

Eight legal firms would handle the class action suit.

It would turn into the third largest medical class action suit in history.

Descent

I imagine the sounds throughout Baybees Pediatrics when it was abuzz with parents and patients. The TV probably blared with kids' cartoons, *the Muppets or Snow White* on the Disney channel. Children's laughter seeps through aging window panes as they play on the merry go round out front on the paved, but crumbling blacktop. Other kids in the waiting room squeal with delight as they play with dolls, stuffed bumble bees and trains.

But always the jolly, jovial, silly music plays in the background and Dr. Bradley sluggishly moves from one exam room to the next. His greasy, shaggy hair and beard have an odor to them like dirty blue jeans. His eyeglasses speckled with tiny spots of dust. He is awkward. Odd. He never looks directly into the eyes of his patients' parents. His blurry, glassy-eyed gaze diverts, always to the babies – to the little girl who has come here today to see Dr. B for her monthly allergy shot or an MMR vaccine.

Bradley's patients later learn that Bradley disseminated tainted or diluted vaccines to hundreds, possibly thousands, of children. No one knows the extent – no one is able to fathom who or how many children were given 'bad' vaccines.

His need to hurt children, to have sexual contact with them, might have begun this way, I imagine. Like any addict, anyone fixated or compulsively obsessed on wrongdoing, he probably thought he could control it, make it submit to him the way he'd most likely submitted to his own uncle or his father who'd probably damaged him as a child, as implied in news articles. But his pathology was so cunning, it fooled him into thinking he was smarter than *it* was. Somewhere, deep inside, whatever goodness was in him would win over evil. He continued to believe this.

Even now.

Over fourteen years after he started.

"Just keep moving," he might have said to himself through gritted teeth as his patient finished tying her red and white sneakers. She sat on the lower level seat of the flowered exam table. The mother might have excused herself to visit the ladies room.

When she returned, Bradley might have suggested she stay in the waiting room while her daughter picked out her toy from the prize room. He smiled heavily. The 'prize room' was located just a few steps away in the "checkerboard" building, located catty-corner to the main practice.

Mom must have felt comfortable enough to wait, to pay her bill or to watch the tail end of *The View or The OPRAH Show*. Before taking the child to the prize room, Bradley might have scooped her up in his arms, swung her around and kissed her cheek again and again. This too had been reported in the papers as Bradley's 'way' with his patients.

Mom was happy when her little girl was happy. She returned Dr. Bradley's smile and probably said, "Great Dr. B," and to her daughter "see you in a while crocodile."

What Else Happened in 2009?

The months of 2010 drift – no – flash by as I write about the case. I think back to what else happened in that same year of his arrest, 2009. It was a time in which a woman named Susan Boyle, too old, too drab, gray haired and frumpy, took the stage on the British version of American Idol, sang like an angel and won; a year of miracles when Captain 'Sully' Sulenberger calmly landed his distressed plane on the frigid Hudson River and saved 155 lives. It was a year when the first black President would make promises of change while a hopeful nation waited and watched.

2009 was also a year of loss; a time in which the U.S. would lose over 4,300 soldiers in the Iraq war which would soon become a war in Afghanistan where they'd lose more. It was a year of massive change: From a rogue author named Sarah Palin who once ran for Vice President to the death of Michael Jackson, to the announcement of the end to a show named simply OPRAH, times changed. A nation grieved for the loss of one of its greatest broadcasters, Walter Cronkite and for the loss of one of its most revered politicians, Edward Kennedy. These events overshadowed the behemoth crimes of Dr. Earl Bradley, in one small town, unless you *lived* in that small town.

2009 was a year in which the Attorney General of Delaware, Beau Biden, would disseminate resources for enraged parents, create task forces, open an outreach building in Lewes and reject his father's senate seat to see the case to its finality. The son of the Vice President of the United States, was sticking with Delaware. He wasn't giving up – not by a long shot.

On Savannah Road

In the Lewes Outreach office at 105 Fourth St and Savannah Rd., the state-operated building becomes a place where parents come to tell their stories, to learn if their child was one of hundreds whom Earl Bradley has so egregiously harmed, to obtain medical records and to get referrals to other pediatricians. In this small five-room, two-story pale yellow cottage-like building, coffee flows continuously as five state employees pour over tens of thousands of medical records ten hours a day, seven days a week.

Ground zero in the war against Bradley.

Here parents find comfort, someone to talk to, someone who knows what is really going on back in the Attorney General's office in Newark, Delaware.

The office happens to be situated only a block from the doctor's home and next door to Beebe Hospital. Beebe: While it has come far in boosting its reputation of a decade ago and has garnered better equipment, better resources, the building itself was still dreary. A faded concrete, beige and pink brick and glass building that looks as though it hasn't been renovated inside the century in which it was built. It has simply grown, taller, wider with a new parking garage stuck onto its side. Inside, I often ask, "Where are the cheery pictures that should be on the walls? Why are the walls painted this sickly yellow, or green? I find the medical staff friendly but…but, I just can't put my finger on what it is that is missing. Something. Perhaps I am just too close to this case to see Beebe, in my mind's eye, without thinking of what Bradley has done to its reputation, to its core.

Bradley's home too, is a faded white, nondescript two-story home that sits on Savannah Road near the hospital and across the street from the Lewes fire house. Labeled an 'historic' home in Lewes, a broken bicycle lay across the front stoop of the raised porch that spreads the width of the house. The "Beware of Dog" sign seems silly, fooling no one.

The authentic coat of armor that once welcomed visitors to the Bradley home has been removed from that front porch. Once upon a time, it signified a man and his family that were just a little whacky, enough so that they'd displayed a welcome sign of a giant coat of armor. No one dares come near the home now – as if it is haunted with the memories of Bradley's crimes. Houses on both sides of his home are also dark – it seems as though no one wants to be associated with him even if they are unlucky enough to live next door.

Later, years after Bradley's arrest, his home, like his office would be covered in weeds and ivy. Broken windows, peeling paint ravage the structure. There is massive shame associated to the house as it begins to crumble, a once-historic structure, one the town will want to tear down, or simply have disappear as if it never existed. Two years after Bradley's arrest, his home goes to auction. No one bids on it. As of October, 2012 the rotting eyesore still sits being eaten away by the relentless weather and vegetation that consumes it.

Birthdays

Monday May 11. It is his birthday today. Earl Bradley is 57 years old. He spends 23 or 24 hours of his days locked in a cell. I often wonder what it must be like for him. What must he think of during his 24 hours day-in and day-out? Does he ever imagine what could have been? A happier life?

One that might have turned out so differently than the one he had.

One where he could have frolicked on the beach with his grandchildren.

One where he could have brought happiness to his business, his friends, his patients.

One where no one would have believed that he was the most hated man in the state.

He is only let out of the secure housing unit for one hour a day at the James T. Vaughn Correctional Center in Smyrna, Delaware about an hour north of Lewes. He is not allowed to exist in the jail's general population. For that hour outside his cell, he can bathe and exercise, alone. He is isolated. Protected from other inmates.

He survives.

Generally, secure housing unit inmates may have visitors, make phone calls and keep a few personal items in their cells. Bradley is allowed four phone calls per month and two 45-minute visits a month. But no one visits except his lawyers. All his meals are served inside his cell. Some inmates in the unit are allowed to have a television or radio that they may listen to only through headphones. Bradley's status does not allow this.

Alone

I do not feel much for him lately. My feelings about him seem to ebb and wane and then go numb. Sometimes I try to feel what he must, but I can't feel his pain or loneliness, certainly I can't imagine his thoughts. Still I am curious. What must he think and do for 16 hours awake on any given day…always, alone? What does he dream at night? What is he doing on his birthday – will it be any different than all the other days? Did he get any calls? From anyone?

I sit on my deck looking over my thriving gardens. The wild rose bushes sing; the giant variegated hoesta have burst from the ground. They are so alive as compared to the doctor who must surely be dead inside by now. I move inside, to think, to write about my thoughts or Bradley's thoughts in jail.

On his birthday.

Terrors

I wonder about what he dreams. Are his dreams all nightmares? Or night terrors? Also known as sleep terrors or *pavor nocturnes*, a night terror is a parasomnia disorder characterized by extreme terror and a temporary inability to regain full consciousness. These dreams are far more dreadful than a nightmare. So dreadful, in fact, that people have sometimes, literally died from them. Does he live these night terrors during the day now too, unable to regain full consciousness even though he is fully awake? Can he tell the difference between his waking hours and night-time terrors any longer? Or might this be wishful thinking on my part?

Some of the adult night terror sufferers have many of the characteristics of abused and depressed individuals including inhibition of aggression, self-directed anger, passivity, anxiety, impaired memory and the ability, eventually, to ignore pain. These terrors are often trauma based. If Bradley does have these night terrors he would most likely wake up abruptly and upon waking might gasp, moan or scream. His arms and legs would flail.

Like the children he harmed.

A Day in a Diner

One of my guilty pleasures is to have a late breakfast at my local diner on any given Saturday afternoon. I have with me a book called *Evil Inside Human Violence and Cruelty*, another paperback I hope will help me understand the evil things people do. As I wait for my breakfast, the book is opened to page 22, I'm also watching the television that is mounted above the doorway. Usually, it is tuned in to Fox News.

This diner comforts me and reminds me of home back on Long Island when I was a little girl. The North Shore, or anywhere on Long Island for that matter, is filled with both large and small diners, with menus ranging from two pages to ten. This diner is on the small, cozy side with its dark blue-purplish carpet, its white-washed wooden walls and Formica table tops. It is decorated with antique lace curtains as if the owners had brought them from the 'old country.' Back in time, from Greece. The comfort, or the memories, might come from the smell of dinner cooking: sizzling onions, heavily spiced vegetables or the garlic and eggplant for tonight's special, Greek Mousakka.

My breakfast is served by the owner's daughter. She is about 25 or 26 and is always ready with a welcoming smile and her "can I get you anything else?" question.

"No thanks. I'm good," comes my reply. As she is walking away and I'm about to dig in to my sausage and eggs, we both stop, her, mid-step, me, mid-bite when the TV News announcer breaks another story about another child molestation case – this time, just outside Philadelphia.

The day outside is one of those perfect, cloudless days with bright, crisp sunshine. It is the kind of day I should be walking 'the boards' in downtown Rehoboth or hiking one of our sandy park trails. It is the kind of day where you would not expect to be eating breakfast at 3pm in a tiny, dark diner and not one of those where you expect to have the conversation that was about to happen.

I will call the mother I spoke with, Kelly. Kelly and I watch the piece on this latest case intently. The Bradley case is still very, very fresh in most minds. We all mumble something about disgusting, and next, the conversation turns to Bradley. I tell her I am trying to chronicle the case, how it affected me and my community. After a bit more small talk about medical care in this area, a bit more complaining and the bitter disgust about Bradley, Kelly tells me:

She'd taken her 3-year-old daughter to see Bradley about two years prior to his arrest.

She'd taken her to see him on *several* occasions.

She'd been new in town and was referred to the only 'near-by' pediatrician.

Her daughter was five now.

Kelly wasn't sure yet, about the damage to her daughter.

She told me how at first, he'd been okay with her, but then seemed to overly dote on her child. Later, the doting turned to…inappropriate.

"Just too much kissing."

Silly laughter, twirling her daughter 'round and around.

Kelly later realized that there was something wrong with Dr. Bradley but couldn't put her finger on it. First she tried to question Bradley: "What are you doing? Why are you touching my daughter that way?" Bradley diverted his eyes, shuffled his feet and abruptly left the room. A confrontation then ensued between a nurse and Kelly when she asked why the doctor would behave this way. The nurse tried to laugh it off, saying how 'affectionate' Bradley was with all his little patients and then told Kelly she was being 'silly.'

Kelly, still feeling something wasn't right, went to the State Police just down the street from Bradley's office. It was Troop 9, the one who would ultimately arrest Bradley two years later. They told her, without hard evidence they could do nothing about a doctor, who by the way, had an outstanding reputation in this area." Kelly was made to feel foolish about her complaints. Still, she was done with Earl Bradley and would drive her daughter the 25 miles it would take to see another pediatrician.

She couldn't have known then, until two years later when she was asked to identify her child in one of the confiscated video's that her child had also been abused by Dr. Bradley.

The diner was quiet on that late Saturday afternoon so Kelly sits with me. We talk for well over an hour; half of it, she is in tears. The other half I am in tears telling her, I am sorry for what her family is having to endure. But she says it is almost a relief to talk about it with someone who wasn't the police, wasn't from the AG's office, wasn't another parent. Someone who would just listen, and be mad as hell for what she and her daughter were going through.

When she was done, she seemed spent – her under-eyes smeared with black mascara, her muscles no longer tight with anger.

I think now of how many of these parents I have met in the most unexpected of ways: In a diner, in line for coffee, in a hair salon, at the dentist's office. How they seem so willing to share their stories about their experience with Bradley. Most of these parents hadn't had to identify their children through 'still photos' taken from the video evidence or testify about Bradley to the state. They are the ones who are 'pretty sure' Bradley did not hurt their children.

I, on the other hand, am not sure at all.

I don't tell them this.

It is not up to me.

Jokes

Late afternoon on another weekend in May and I am home re-reading some articles on the case. Although it is Springtime, the crisp evening air feels like winter. It sneaks in through the screen door in the sunroom, left slightly ajar like a refrigerator door left open.

In this particular article, we, the followers of the case, learn more – about what was said or done in the past; who knew what, when; why no one knew *not* to take their kids to Dr. Earl Bradley.

It is reported in this article that another parent said she informed the Medical Board in 2005. It was never followed through. The case was dropped because the {then} Attorney General, Jane Brady, said there wasn't enough evidence for an arrest, that "They couldn't win the case." So the abuse continued. From 2005 to 2009, none of the parents who saw Bradley knew about these complaints to the law, the Medical Society, the Board or about issues at Beebe Medical Center. How could they? Damned privacy laws.

Even *I* cannot believe how many times I have read and re-read the fact that, investigations and suspicions about Bradley were dropped or weren't taken far enough. I return again and again, in my head, to that Dr. Phil Show where he spoke of how many times Bradley got away with what he did – how many times did the system have to fail before he would be caught? Two years later in 2012 the Penn State-Sandusky case would be compared to *that pediatrician in Delaware* case in magazines or news articles. Where and when will it end I ask over and over?

I return to the article: In one police affidavit, a detective wrote that two pediatricians told officers about complaints from patients who transferred out of Bradley's practice in 2005. Two separate doctors said this? I could almost understand one doctor making this statement, but two? Why I ask again, wasn't this followed through with? I think again how one of those pediatricians, Dr. Scott, worked with Bradley for a short period of time and said he'd often referred "jokingly" about Bradley as a pedophile when talking to colleagues. That doctor also said three former patients of Bradley's had similar stories about him conducting long vaginal exams. He was just "joking around?"

How much truth can be found in jokes? If there's even a trace of truth in regard to such an ugly situation, it's not funny. People tend to turn ugly situations or hints of suspicion into a joke when they are uncomfortable and they're having trouble processing the truth. "Oh I was just kidding." But they're not.

Why would anyone refer to a fellow doctor as a pedophile if there wasn't a *reason* for calling him this? Perhaps this horrendous situation could have been stopped had it been confronted, had it *not* been made into a silly joke.

The article goes on to talk more about other parents who said Bradley kissed their kids obsessively. I felt like I stepped into an alternative universe reading this, after Kelly had, just days before, told me her story about Bradley's obsessive kissing. In the paper, I read that this father swore he saw Bradley, on one occasion, stick his tongue in his child's mouth, but it happened so quickly, like the flutter of a hummingbird's wing, that he couldn't trust what he'd seen. He couldn't believe what his own mind had just witnessed.

When Dr. Scott was asked *why* he didn't report the things he'd seen or heard about Bradley, he said his comment {about Bradley being a pedophile} had been taken out of context and that he couldn't say more. "I've been subpoenaed," he explained. The law is clear that if you, as a medical professional, even *suspect* fraud or the misuse of power by a medical professional, the physicians' oath says you have a duty to report this to the state medical board.

A Duty:

To heal.

To protect.

Medical staff can be fined $10,000 if they don't.

I find that "national studies and lawsuit records suggest that sexual molestation by doctors is all too frequent." One recent study finds nearly one in 10 complaints relating to sexual misconduct.

In 2009 for instance, there were a total of 565 complaints made to the Board of Medical Practice in Delaware. This number will double in only the first part of 2010, because of what Bradley did.

Of those 565 only 25 of them were related to a sexual complaint. Only half of the 25 were given any disciplinary action for sexual misconduct. Only half I ask?

Chaperone

Another question frequently asked: "Why wasn't there another medical staffer in the room during Bradley's exams? Isn't this some law, or some policy?"

Still in research mode, I Google medical policies and up pops The American Medical Association which, in short, says "The use of a chaperone during physical exams provides reassurance to patient; a witness is available to support the physician's innocence should a misunderstanding or false accusation be made and it offers advantages in convenience and time efficiency when authorized health professionals serve as chaperones and can assist with procedures such as gynecological exams."

It goes on to say: *"...would like to remind health providers of the importance of having a chaperone during physical examinations."* I learn it is important because there is a varying sense of invasiveness during different types of physical exams and those 'feelings' can vary among patients. But there is a general consensus that an exam of the reproductive organs (pelvic, testicular, breasts, rectum) <u>heightens the importance of a chaperone.</u>

Still, even though the use of a chaperone is highly recommended by the AMA, Bradley never had another adult in the room during his exams – until forced to by Beebe Hospital and only then when the nurse reported Bradley's 'inappropriate' catheterizations on young girls. I can't help but ask: Didn't the very idea that the hospital imposed the use of a chaperone on Bradley trigger any thoughts of looking further into his background? Or to question his practices? His medical standards?" My understanding is that hospitals don't usually do thorough background checks when hiring new physicians; they simply make sure the license is up to date and there are no 'marks' against him. This non-thorough checking into a doctor's background would greatly change after Bradley's conviction.

At Beebe hospital an official said that the restriction of using a chaperone with Bradley was prompted by "vague rumors about alleged incidents" in Pennsylvania and an investigation in Milford. And so in a sense, Beebe's failure in reporting what they *suspected* kept Bradley supplied with victims for years. "Vague rumors – alleged incidents?" These words echo in my ears like a funeral dirge.

In response to their apparent inaction to report Bradley, the hospital later stated "though we don't generally operate on such rumors, out of an abundance of caution we felt it prudent to require Dr. Bradley to have a chaperone whenever seeing patients inside the hospital. He was notified of this requirement and readily consented."

This same article reported that "The hospital further stated that back in 2005 they didn't realize they had a 'responsibility' to report what they had heard about Bradley."

Yet, the mere fact that a doctor would _need_ to work under a chaperone's supervision clearly indicates, at the very least,

the need for more research,

the need to look deeper into Dr. Earl's Bradley's background.

Should he have even been hired in the first place? While I understand that no medical institution or corporation or human being is perfect, weren't there clear signs to hospital administration that there were major problems with Bradley? Were they so desperate because of lower scales, making it more difficult to entice medical personnel to practice here in Delaware? Couldn't they see? I am tired now – my faith feels damaged. I leave the papers and news clippings scattered all over my desk. All over the floor.

Failures

Who knew what, when, about Bradley?

Initially, Beebe officials insisted they had no knowledge until his arrest.

But they *knew* police had seized some of the hospital files on Bradley during an earlier investigation.

Initially, the hospital denied knowledge of wrongdoing by Bradley.

It wasn't only Beebe who didn't, *initially*, come forward or who didn't take action. There were others: Other doctors, nurses, former office managers, office staffers, even some parents who complained about Bradley, who said he was so adept at manipulation that they questioned themselves or delayed reporting what they had witnessed.

One mother said she didn't immediately report him because her family feared no one would believe her accusations.

I think there is such grave sadness in people's fear. For it was fear that stopped so many from coming forward. Fear that no one would listen or that they'd mistakenly accuse a well-respected doctor. Fear of retribution.

So many fears, yet isn't the fact that no one came forward in itself, as neglectful as the civil suits allege? Isn't their failure to act, as sinful as the motorists who kept driving and did nothing to help the 26 year old girl in Toledo, or the pedestrians who heard cries for help from a New York City window and never called police?

Suddenly I feel guilt at my own finger-pointing. My little tantrum that sounds to my own ears like a lecture of some sort. Would *I* have been brave enough? Enough? I assume Yes but would *I* have followed through or would fear have prevented me too – from stopping or even reporting this madman; how easy it is, to turn a blind eye or not *want* to see the truth.

Molested

Molestation. Such a polite word for rape.

I am thinking again about what he might have been like in his office, during a typical workday at Baybees. How and when he decides he will molest a child; why he can't stop what he is about to do.

I imagine an early September morning, a cool sunny day. The summer crowds have gone home so the doctor is free to concentrate on his regular patients now. He wouldn't have to cram in all those strangers who'd come to his practice, whose kids had some silly earache or broken arm. Bradley would see Mom and daughter Sondra (a fictitious name) in the "Ariel the Mermaid" exam room which is colorful and cheery. I imagine Mom stays close by as mothers usually do. This is only her third – or was it her fourth? – visit to see Dr. Bradley at Baybees. Her daughter is 3 years old.

Does he ask himself, is it time yet? Does Mom trust him enough? Does her daughter?

Bradley has become brasher by 2009. After all they hadn't caught him in earlier investigations. By 2009 he wouldn't just stop, he would leap over his own boundaries as to when and where he'd touch a child. He has become more reckless, more impatient. I imagine his urges have become harder to control. In the past, he made sure the parents trusted, even adored him, made sure the child was so comfortable she couldn't resist going to the prize room. This too is part of his scheme, and it's not as if the 'prizes' were some Dollar Store cheap junk he'd bought either. He had hundreds of toys, most costing upwards of $10 - $20 each. One Dad even asked him how he could afford lavishing such extravagant gifts on his patients. He probably saw over 50 patients a week. "What was up with that?" the father asked. Bradley pushed him off with a flippant answer of how he got the toys wholesale. The parent seemed satisfied. He didn't ask again.

Even at wholesale prices though, doctors in Southern Delaware don't have that kind of money to spend on their patients. Even though it is a top resort area in season, it is still a small, rural area where Bradley tended to patients, year-round – a place surrounded by small farms, people who work at the local chicken processing plants and family-owned businesses. Although there are plenty of mini-mansions and luxury condominiums, it is still considered small town living with its tree-lined streets and very little crime.

But Earl Bradley makes the toys, the child rides, the lollipops and dolls his way to lure the children – to make them feel safe when they hold his hand and visit the prize room in the checker-board building. They are only gone for a few minutes. He makes sure the parents never come looking for their children.

Kisses

On that day in September, I imagine that Bradley slathers big wet kisses on Sondra's cheek. The child might have looked up at him with quiet, trusting brown eyes. He then asks her mother if it is OK to take her to the prize room. "Sondra deserves it. She is *so* special." Because Mom had been given the tour of the grounds several months ago on one of her first visits, she probably feels comfortable letting the doctor take her child away for only a few moments to pick out her toy.

"We'll back in a jiffy," he says.

And off they go.

They might have returned in under six minutes. Maybe four. But what happens in those minutes is unspeakable.

It takes less than a minute to reach the underground area of the checker-board 'out house' next door. Perhaps he is playful making Sondra laugh. Do they skip, even hop, into the building, down the stairs, holding hands, together?

Does Bradley's chest tighten with heavy breathing, as mine is right now trying to picture this? Does he feel a tingling sensation in his hands or feet - in his groin as they reach the bottom of the stairs? I imagine it is dark inside this basement area. I know from what I've heard – there is this dark gray couch across from the oak stairway, an old, metal office desk, a ratty chair and a desktop computer. Perhaps a single ceiling bulb lights the area. What few windows exist in the room are covered with dark heavy drapes. They are headed for the other side of the room where it is more cheery; more welcoming to the children: A yellow shag rug, a small round tea table and three small wooden chairs. I imagine.

But that dark gray couch. I do not have to imagine this couch – It is where several of his attacks took place and nine months later, at another court hearing where Bradley's lawyers would challenge the search and seizure of evidence, I'd see a photo of this couch. I will never forget that image.

There are no other pictures of the basement so I still have to imagine Disney toys perched on every shelf, everywhere. And the candy. Bowls and jars filled with every kind of candy imaginable; and lollipops. It is a kids' wonderland.

Except for the ever-ready video camera poised and positioned, ready to capture the moment with just a touch of the button.

From what I've heard and read, video evidence might have shown Sondra touching or stroking the toys, trying to decide which one to take home. Suddenly, Bradley grabs her by the shoulders and twirls her around so she faces him — she stands eye level just above his knees.

His voice might have been difficult to understand. The video image is muffled but still audible. Bradley says as he bends over, stroking her hair. "Dr. B needs you to do something that will make him feel good," he says. He holds her too tight and she tries to squirm away, ducking under his arms. He grabs her again. Dr. B. is angry now.

"Sondra, what did I just say to you? We don't have much time."

"I don't want to help you Dr. B," she says. Her eyes and voice are tinged with fear now.

"Don't tell your Mommy or Daddy about this. It's special. Just between us."

This next part I didn't have to imagine as some images reviewed by forensics investigators were leaked. It is said Bradley becomes violent, enraged, grabbing the still-struggling girl by her ankles and pulling her down to the floor. The camera angle would be just right, he might have thought. The doctor quickly takes the little girl from behind as her screams pierce the damp basement air. When he penetrates her, his eyes are filled with rage; seemingly, he has no control, almost like a drunk in a black-out. He pushes and pushes while at the same time holding his big burley arms around her head and over her face, almost smothering her. Her screams became muffled whimpers.

Symbols

"Tear it down!" scream letters from readers of the local Gazette newspaper. "Bradley's place should be razed – Enough!" The signs, the shack-like buildings, the bumble-bee painted cars and the bronze statues stand like a billboard of terror, reminders of what Bradley did. To the town. To the families. And to their kids.

Every day as people drive by the play-land practice, they are forced to think about Bradley's crimes against a gentle community. "My heart and my prayers reach out to all the victims. I hope our community will agree with me that the victims deserve the removal of the buildings so that the families and our entire community can begin to heal," says one of the letters that appears in the paper. The giant sign that reads Baybees Pediatrics stands approximately 25 feet x 15 feet high – as big as the building itself. No one needs this symbol – this reminder of the pain they live with daily.

Another letter to the editor says, "In conversation with others, I personally refuse to call him 'doctor' anymore. Only respected people deserve that title. My wish is for the authorities to collect any evidence they need and then set a date for removal of the buildings. Whether it be a bulldozer or an implosion, just get rid of the constant reminder of the horrors that were committed."

One member of the town erects black crosses on the site and ties black ribbons on the railings at the buildings' entrance. One day, hidden inside one of the black ribbons, a reporter finds a note from a mother, one who wishes to remain anonymous. Her child, another one of Bradley's victims. The note speaks of untold heartache and how she wishes Bradley dead.

Finally, in the Spring of 2010, the hideous 'symbols' of Bradley's crimes are removed from sight. The buildings, although beginning to decay, must remain standing for now. But the cars, the toys and the statues of super-heroes, are hidden away behind fences in the corner of his property, behind giant weeds and bushes. It had only been four weeks since the 'tear it down' outcries began. It felt like a life-time to the victim families. The little carousel was boarded up, the bronze ring-around-the-rosie children removed, the gigantic sign pulled down by crane. In this day of legal complexities and the constitutional guarantee that all those charged are innocent until proven guilty, gaining consent for the removal of these items was no easy feat. Tearing the buildings down would be another.

But it's done. You can almost hear the collective sigh of relief from an angry community.

Porn

Still thousands of cars pass by the pediatrician's buildings each day.

Still, parents are anxious as they search for answers.

They hear that their babies might be on the internet now, how pedophiles often share their pictures.

When I think of his crimes and his victims' images possibly being shared on the internet, my gut clenches. I know that 40,000 images of child porn are posted on-line every week along with the appearance of at least twenty new children. The appetite for babies as young as four months old has soared. Many of these children have been kidnapped and sold into pedophile rings. I can barely bring myself to keep reading about this sick world of pedophilia.

If

Officials on the case expect more charges to come against Bradley and are still reaching out to parents as they gather information and continue to identify the children in the videos.

If found guilty, Bradley faces life in prison. *If.* Even with 14 hours of documented 'proof,' even with multiple witnesses, he is still innocent until proven guilty.

My stomach churns as I write.

Writing

My spot to write about Earl Bradley is my writing desk in the small library just steps inside the front door of my home. A cubby hole of sorts – only 10'x12', painted deep red with built-in book shelves. The room is sparsely decorated with few distractions. My golden retriever sleeps half in, half out of the doorless entry-way to my library.

Because the room is just steps away from the front door, I shudder each time the doorbell rings. What if a neighbor or a not-so-close friend looks at my writing desk, littered with news articles, books and magazine articles piled on top of each other? These things almost obscure the family picture and large candle at each end of my desk. And the desk clutter is about nothing but Bradley, other pedophile cases, and child trauma. If my neighbors or friends were to lift their eyes from the bizarre articles on my desk, they'd see the news clippings taped to the shelves. They'd see pictures of Dr. Bradley. One of him before his arrest: clean cut, beardless with a slight smile. The second photo is Bradley about two months after the arrest in jail, scraggly beard, slovenly, dead eyes.

These pictures taped to my shelves remind me of a crime scene bulletin board. He lives there. On my desk, on my shelves and in my library.

He is a part of my life.

I've grown used to him now, used to him being there, like you get used to a picture on a wall, a pile of tax papers sitting in a corner. But sometimes my work on the pedophile takes over my head and my usually happy demeanor is replaced by a dark negative one. But this is only sometimes. Most often, Bradley is just a character in a book to me now. I compartmentalize him, as I would characters in a novel. I can think about him and even talk about him as if he were any ordinary joe walking down the street. Any ordinary man with four beautiful kids, an ex-wife and a dog living in lovely downtown Lewes. It is only when I start talking about him to those who ask questions about the case, that I realize how casual I must sound. I hear myself speaking awful phrases: "almost killed five of the 100 children; sodomized with bottle heads; molested children younger than 6 months old...." and even to my own ears, I sound heartless and cold.

Yesterday, another warm spring day I was stuck in Dover, Delaware buying a new car. As I wait for a deal to be struck, I start a casual conversation with two car dealers. And somehow, I wind up telling these strangers that I am writing the story of the doctor pedophile from Lewes. They are both male, both in their late thirties, both fathers. One leans back in his chair, his feet propped on the desk, the other leans on his desk, head in hand. They seem comfortable, laid back.

Until I bring up the Bradley details. The one, chin in hand, sits up straight. The other one removes his feet from the desk. Two sets of eyes widen, eyebrows raised and they are strictly focused on me. I tell the Bradley story and answer their questions – the same first question as always, "Where were the parents?" whom I immediately defend. One man listens intently, asking questions. He slides his chair closer now in an attempt to learn more. The other keeps scrunching up his face, shaking his shoulders and finally just walks away, making grunting, ugly sounds as he does so. I believe he makes these sounds in distaste of Bradley's crimes - but another part of me thinks, maybe he thinks *I* am the distasteful one.

Behind my laptop in my library lay articles about crimes other than Bradley's, that have happened here in Sussex County. Since the doctor's case broke in December of 2009 there occurred the tragic story of a father killing his nineteen year-old son just twenty minutes from my house; then left the boy's body to rot in the back yard. Another story emerges about a teacher and football coach at Cape Henlopen High School also located in Lewes, who was caught raping and possibly torturing a sixteen year old girl from his own school. It's as if the Bradley case has opened up something awful in our town – exposed us to so much more than just his own story.

Another article with the headline *Shattered Faith*, talks about the Wisconsin priest, Father Murphy, who allegedly molested scores of deaf boys. Apparently the head of the Catholic Church knew about it and did nothing.

It all sounds too familiar. Suspicions, rumors and still, no one tells.

In the photo of the victim in the priest story, the man stands with his hands folded over his chest. Sixty-one now, he was molested when he was 12. "It stays with you your entire life."

It is the same thing my 72 year-old neighbor told me; the same thing another friend said who'd been molested when she was 13. Under this particular pile of articles is another article torn from PEOPLE Magazine titled "A Family of Monsters" which relates the story of a Midwestern town in turmoil after siblings say they were assaulted by six male relatives more than 20 years ago. "Their father forced them to watch him sodomize their brother as one punishment." This, plus charges of rape, sodomy and even bestiality carried out between 1980 and 1996. Again, why in so many cases, does it take the victims fourteen, twenty, thirty years to come forward? Why does it take them so long to lift their burden? Massive shame, which should not be, fear of reprisal from the predator, fear for their own safety and that of their families. Some, perhaps many, were too young to understand what had happened to them. These then, are the secrets that cripple lives.

Five more recent news articles are scattered to the left of the laptop – not filed, just thrown. And under them is the original loose leaf binder where I *used to be* organized: newspaper clippings neatly placed in a black binder; downloaded blogs in a digital Bradley file; other articles about similar cases in a yellow basket. On top of the binder are scattered some yellow index cards from my 'thought box' where I write ideas for new scenes in the middle of the night, in the middle of a TV show, in the middle of a book I'm reading. I never knew when I first began this project what it meant to be so obsessed with something. I never knew that it would literally impact almost every facet of my life. Or I'd forgotten what obsessions were like. Not since being a young woman in my teens or twenties who was obsessed with horses or skiing or boys, had I been so consumed. The kind of obsession that obliterates everything else. Is this part of what I like so much about writing this story?

AG Biden

Sometimes I get so tired and ask myself, Why am I putting myself through this? The sadness of writing all these pages about a sick doctor drains me. What keeps me going? I seem to ask this question more and more the further along I get in telling the story of this local tragedy. When do the pieces of the puzzle come together?

Will they ever? But certain things, including a phone message from Attorney General Beau Biden, keep me focused.

After visiting the states' office in downtown Lewes, I emailed a letter to Beau Biden. I told him how impressed I was with the Deputy Attorney General, Patricia Dailey Lewis, who ran the office; I told him too how impressed I was with the forums he'd held, as well as his laser focus on this case to the point of giving up the senate seat, his father's senate seat. I told him that I could only imagine this being one of the most difficult decisions in his career. I told him I understood this dark journey of taking down Bradley because, in a different way, it had become my journey too.

In the letter I told the Attorney General I was grateful for his efforts on behalf of the victims. I told him I thought the people of Delaware would never forget it. I also attached the poem I'd chosen to use in a part of this book about protecting the children. ... *"And storms that cross our great nation sometimes pass through here. But here we remain, one place, one people and here we will keep and protect the most precious part of all creation... our beloved children."*

The next morning, a Friday, I missed the phone call, but Attorney General Biden left me a message. I was stunned. I played his message over and over. I could not stop staring at the phone receiver. While I was surprised he called me personally, his call made me realize my email had struck a chord.

"Hi Meg, this is Beau Biden calling. I'm just calling to thank you for your kind email - it meant a great deal to me."

He spoke of his office's perseverance, how they would "keep at this and do their jobs." He then repeated that my words meant a great deal to him, 'more than I knew' and thanked me again.

Now I think of Biden's message when my friends ask "Why are you putting yourself through this?" Or when someone who knows I'm writing this story says to me "Are you trying to *profit* from this story? Or when my neighbor simply asks, "Why?"

I listen to Biden's voice mail and it inspires me. I suppose it gives me hope. I suppose it lets me know I'm not alone.

Grief

There is a sacredness in tears.
They are not the mark of weakness but of power.
They are messengers of overwhelming grief
and of unspeakable love.
　　　　　　　　–Washington Irving

Finding Meaning

Dusk darkens the night as magenta cloud-filled skies give way to grey ones. I return to my writing after a quick walk with Kelly and Maggie. I am thinking of the word I stumbled across the other day - a word that describes what I have witnessed and contemplated for many months now.

Pareidolia describes the human tendency to find meaning where there isn't any.

Isn't that what I had been doing all this time? Searching for the how and why of it all? And now there is an actual word – although Webster's dictionary couldn't find it. But Wikipedia does. I'd searched for its meaning after reading it somewhere. A book? A magazine? I can't remember.

Pareidolia applies to finding an image of the Virgin Mary in a water stain or seeing the face of the man in the moon. Can it also explain the actions of a child predator? Why he did what he did? Does a reason exist at all? We want our world to be both known and mysterious at the same time. Or do we?

Pareidolia.

One little word meaning to find reason in things where no basis, purpose, or answer exists. It is a relatively obscure word that I learned few other people had heard of. The word somehow comforts me. It means that others may be as curious as I, to continually search for reasons when there may be none.

Still, I keep searching. Even with the thousand scalpel-edged memories I'd scraped myself with over the past months, I look for *my* pareidolia. Always I ask myself *why*.

Clues

Recently, a new clue came across my desk. Google alerted me to a 'hit' from AP, the Associated Press in, of all places, some Arizona newspaper. The article began "Former Delaware pediatrician Earl Bradley is also a benefactor of a foundation that helps families grieving the loss of a child." I read that in 2005 Bradley helped members of his family set up a foundation to help pay funeral expenses for families suffering the loss of a newborn or stillborn baby. 2005? I thought. Wasn't this the very same year all the suspicions culminated in the hospitals investigating him as well as the police?

Our local media had reported every single detail that could find on Bradley. Why not this? It was important wasn't it? Perhaps it was something reporters hadn't picked up on, especially with the gag order having been imposed. Or the approaching trial. Or perhaps the hospital's foundation didn't want it reported. More incongruities. More inconsistencies.

Why, I asked, had this journalist from the AP gone to all the trouble, the time, the research - to learn more about Bradley? And then I remember: Dr. Bradley treated patients from all over the country. All over the world. Perhaps this particular writer had taken his little girl to see Bradley many years ago while here on vacation.

Perhaps he lived here once.

I found this item about Bradley's involvement in such a foundation, strange. Chilling, in fact - that he'd start a foundation that donated money toward families who'd lost children. Was this done out of guilt? Maybe, for once in his life, he tried. Maybe he tried to change it all back, like it had never happened, to *fix* what he'd done, to cover it up with something good?

Within this same article a Dr. Fred Berlin, founder of the Johns Hopkins Sexual Disorders Clinic, was interviewed and said "Human beings are simply not black and white - it's not unusual for criminals, even those such as Bradley convicted of monstrous crimes, to have some positive character traits and to have done some good things."

I remind myself that Bradley was once a father, a brother, at one-time, a highly-respected pediatrician, an ordinary human being. Maybe he did do something good. Did this mean at one time he did, in fact, have a conscience?

Darkness

I saw Bev today. She works at the grocery store across the highway and knows I'm writing Bradley's story. I told a friend who works at the store that I was writing about Bradley and was introduced to Bev soon afterward. Bev is tall, salt and pepper shoulder length hair, pale, bony hands. She always seemed sad to me, crushed by something, although early on, I didn't know what.

Once Bev understood the research I'd done on the case, on him - and how many families had been horribly affected, I think she might have felt safe sharing her story with me. I think she just needed someone removed from the emotion of it, to listen. Sometimes it's hard to hear these stories: How she waits, and waits, to learn if her child is one of Bradley's victims; the effects on her family, the overwhelming anger.

"You know, they're saying there's no one who doesn't know someone affected by this thing," she says. Her body seems to slump as she says it. Her eyes turn dark and miserable.

"I know," I say. I heard the same thing around town.

"Have you heard anything yet," I ask then. "About your daughter?" I know the state is still moving through the identification process and then notifying parents. Once state officials review the files and compare those files to pictures of the children, they notify the parents, one by one. Bev tells me that the Lewes Office told her that "no news is good news" at this point. Every day, for weeks, a team of State Police detectives arrive at a different front door on the same heartbreaking mission. They bring with them a carefully cropped video image showing nothing but a young face. That face confirms another family's nightmare: Their child too was another victim of Earl Bradley's. Bev is terrified that her daughter who had seen Bradley numerous times between the age of one and eight years old, will be one of those identified.

For three weeks, after delivering three different pictures of her daughter at various ages, Bev waited to see if her daughter was one of the children identified by Biden's office. She is having trouble getting out of bed some days; other days she can't bear thinking about going to work. She is so preoccupied. She waits for word. She can't stop crying. She doesn't want her daughter to know, even if Bev finds out her daughter is one of them. Her daughter is eight now. And yet: "What if she is one of them he'd touched but didn't film? How will I ever know?" Bev asked.

"Do you really want to know?" I ask. "Some parents I've met don't want to…." Quite simply, they want to live with the hope that their child was too young to remember, that their child's future won't be negatively affected by this or that *their* child might have been one of the lucky ones.

"I know the bastard targeted her," Bev said now. "And God, when I look back on so many things, there were signs but those signs never added up. Not then. But damn that fucking bastard. They do now!" We share a glance, the briefest of eye-taps. There is a greater, angrier brittleness about her now. Her entire body vibrates like a tuning fork.

"How do you mean," I ask, while standing in a quiet corner near the fresh produce area. We are still inside the store. I watch as everyday shoppers chat with one another, pick out their cereal or cheese or canned goods.

"We first started seeing him when she was only three and he'd asked her after several visits if she wanted to go to the candy room – she said 'no.' So we went with her. At first, he was all animated and proud to show off the different exam rooms, or his prize (candy) room. Smiling, all happy-like. But, on the way back, he was different, distant, almost angry. I think that day he targeted her and wanted to be alone with her."

Bev continues, "She saw him six days before the arrest. It was for a urinary tract infection." Bev looked at me again, this time with sad, glassy eyes, head cast down. It is all about grief now. And hope.

I think of that beautiful sentence I read once a long time ago, by Emily Dickenson: "Hope is the thing with feathers that perches in the soul, and sings the tune without words and never stops at all."

I find out later that Bev no longer works at the grocery store. A mutual friend said she'd heard Bev's family got the call. Bev quit her job the following day.

Anger

"What the hell are you talking about...he knew exactly what he was doing!"

Another group of three has gathered at Starbucks, in line waiting for their coffee. Another, breezy, late-spring-time day, and the Starbucks on Route 1 is packed.

"If he's pleading mental insanity, that means he didn't know what he was doing or wasn't in "his right mind," says the guy in khaki shorts and a striped Polo shirt.

"Well, that's bullshit. Every day for like ten years? And he didn't know? Get out, he –"

"Maybe his legal guy will go for diminished capacity. I don't know but somebody should just shoot the schmuck and put us all out of our misery."

Of course I know who they are talking about. Yes, another day at Starbucks or another day at the grocery or a day at Arena's Deli where they talk; where friends grow angry with one another, where neighbors debate what will happen to Earl Bradley.

At first, in the early weeks after his arrest, groups talked about "why the children hadn't said anything or about why the parents hadn't been with their children every second." Now that Bradley has been indicted the talk in town is about his lawyer and what defense he'll present. It was reported he would go for mental insanity. Then the townsfolk ask, "How the *hell* could any lawyer take this case?"

I could butt into their conversation but I don't. If I had I would have told them that Bradley's (original) lawyer was the top criminal defense attorney in the state: Gene Maurer. He is best known for taking on the famous murder case of Thomas Capano and Steven Pennell, Delaware's only documented serial killer. The state of Delaware hired

Maurer to prosecute Pennell so the conviction would be upheld. Apparently a smart move by the state. Many years ago Maurer traveled around the country to learn more about DNA evidence since this case was one of the first to allow DNA to be used as evidence in a murder trial. Friends of mine know Maurer and describe him as affable, skilled and highly respected in his field; other descriptions I read said this: "He's sharp, in every sense of the word: His intellect, his tone, his mouth."

I remind myself that even Bradley is entitled to a defense. That everyone under the constitution is entitled. In the same breath I think about asking Maurer "How can you defend him?" As any top lawyer might answer, he'd say "A good defense lawyer never forgets his client is a human being, no matter how overwhelming the evidence of guilt."

This might be the only thing that made Bradley worth defending.

Later, we'd find out that Maurer drops the case and lets the public defender take over.

Bradley had no money to pay a private lawyer.

Insanity

The not guilty by reason of insanity defense came to be in 1843 when a person named M'Naghten traveled to 10 Downing Street in London to ambush then Prime Minister Robert Peel but mistakenly shot and killed Peel's secretary. During the ensuing trial, several psychiatrists testified that M'Naghten was delusional. A jury agreed, declaring him not guilty by reason of insanity, and *voila!* a legal standard came to be that has been used in the court system for the last 150 years. The rule says the defendant may be acquitted only if they labored "under such defect of reason from disease of the mind" as to not realize what he was doing or why it was a crime.

The insanity defense is an attempt to impose a moral check on a system largely designed to weigh facts and evidence. Thus, it allows judges and juries to decide some defendants aren't "criminally responsible" for their actions even though those acts might be a crime under different circumstances. Take John Hinckley, convicted of attempting to shoot then President Reagan in 1981; or John Wayne Gacy, arrested in 1978. Gacy was the successful businessman who hired young men, and then raped, murdered and buried them under his house. Both successfully used the insanity defense in their cases.

Some states have abolished the use of an insanity defense, an action upheld by the U.S. Supreme Court in 1994. Some have amended their laws to include standards of "diminished capacity" or "guilty but mentally ill," but these laws still have roots in the "M'Naghten rule." Other rules define the plea as "guilty but not criminally responsible by reason of insanity." However, "mental disease or illness alone does not constitute a legal insanity defense."

Another tactic the defense may consider is that Bradley understood his behavior was criminal but he was "unable to control it." This is sometimes called the "irresistible impulse" defense.

Bradley might resist such a defense and simply plead guilty. Even if he's found to have diminished capacity, even if it's ruled he couldn't control himself, what will that prove?

It won't win him his freedom. It won't win him hope.

While many are calling for the death penalty for Bradley, the death penalty in Delaware is reserved solely for murder. In 2010 only twelve states do *not* allow the death penalty.

Delaware is not one of them.

Part III: Summer/Fall 2010

Thomas Hardy once wrote "And yet, to every bad, there is a worse."

The hot, steamy months of summertime are upon us. Memorial Day weekend has arrived and with it, 100,000 tourists race to the beaches of Rehoboth and Lewes. They stream past the new 'eye in the sky' surveillance cameras to catch speeders crashing through the red lights at the end of the street where I live, Old Landing Road. Another 'gotcha light' is just past Old Landing at Munchy Branch and Rt. 1.

These cameras are mounted on large electric poles on the Coastal Highway just a mile before hitting the left turn to downtown Rehoboth. It is the stretch of road where drivers become their most impatient in their last few minutes before reaching the beach. The cameras continually flash, like lightning striking the air, again and again as summer tourists try to beat the light that stalls them from reaching the beach sixty seconds sooner. The ticket for racing the light is $110. On this Memorial Day Weekend, Sussex County will make upwards of $40,000 off the new digital cops.

Most of these tourists are unaware of what happened in these small towns over the past six months. While they are unaware of what happened here, they would remember the great blizzards of this winter, the awful oil spill in the gulf or the murder of Yeardley Love by George Huguely, the young UVA star lacrosse player. But the story of Earl Bradley, the serial baby molester, is unknown to most. They run to their vacations. Their children lick their ice cream cones and chomp on chips in the back seat of their mini-vans that crawl to the seaside. Most of these vehicles driving southbound on Route 1 passed his boarded up practice. But they are unaware. The giant sign above the building, reads *Antiques* now. It too is torn, faded, ripped and appears to be exactly what it is: The sign that lay dormant, underneath the Baybees Pediatrics sign of Dr. Earl Bradley.

Because most of these tourists are unaware of what has happened here, they might envy us for living here.

But we envy them for what they do *not* know.

Abandoned

Small drops of summer rain pelt my car's windshield as I sit outside Bradley's old practice on Route 1. Something drove me to visit these boarded up buildings today – again - seven months since the crimes occurred. My air conditioning whirs in the background and I type on my laptop. My stomach churns. My SUV's car doors are locked. I am anxious sitting here just eight feet from the front steps of the checker-board building where his attacks on at least 127 children - that we know of - took place.

Eighty degrees outside on this hot muggy day and yet I feel icy cold. I am having trouble understanding why I'm so nervous. I feel slimy being here. Uncomfortable. Again, I think why? Do I just feel silly sitting in my car writing about a crazed baby molester? Am I even permitted to be on this property? Am I breaking the law somehow? I realize, finally, it is the first time, perhaps ever, that I've been in the presence of evil. And known about it.

Baybees Pediatrics appears more forsaken, even more foreboding than before. What little grass there is alongside the cracked black top parking lot is four feet high and sprouts buds on top. It is unnerving being here – this complete and utter abandonment of this property. I keep looking in my rear-view mirror. What am I waiting for? Is the place under surveillance? Will some vision of Bradley appear from behind one of the windows that is covered with a dirty sheet?

I tell myself I am being paranoid. He's in jail for heaven's sake! The two buildings and small shack-like structures are barely standing. They are even more dilapidated than before. I peer around the side of the car listening for another car, some sound. It is eerily quiet. I think what is also making me nervous is that I feel haunted by the depravity of what happened here – something unthinkable.

The black ribbons tied to the porch columns flap in the wind - ghostlike now. My cell phone rings and I jump an inch off the car seat. A loud yelp escapes my lips as I grab for the phone. Breathless, I bark "hello!" and it takes me a moment to get my breathing under control.

Rusting wires hang off the main building of the practice, as if someone pulled all the plugs or cut them. Then there is the white building catty-corner to the main one, the one painted in a checker-board design. It is the most eerie of them all with the black against the white symbolizing yet another child's game: That of checkers. It is where most of the rapes took place, downstairs on that dark grey couch.

Chipped and peeling paint is seen on almost every corner of the three buildings that stand in an L shape. Nothing has been touched here in more than six months. I wonder if I might be the only one who has dared to park on these grounds since the arrest.

Other than the cops,

Or the Mom who tied the black ribbons

Or the construction workers who, by instruction from the AG's office, rid the place of Bradley's toys and beat-up old cars.

Who else would come here?

Who would dare?

My eyes dart around the property again and I see his play things: The two yellow and black VW bugs painted like bumble bees, the children's Ferris wheel, the Buzz Lightyear figure thrown on top of one of the cars, little bumblebee toys and a black and yellow colored swing seat – all have been tossed in a junk pile behind the shed. Grass grows around and through the items. Out of public sight. Almost. Although everything was thrown behind a dilapidated privacy fence, it too is pitted and rotting. And so the trash can still be seen, a garbage dump of junk thrown into a heap some 8 feet high. I am reminded of the lives tossed into one big heap; of the spirits lost; of the civil and class action law suits and the possible job loss by hospital employees. The possible loss of the hospital all together. All those parents and their children possibly leaving the area, the effects on the schools...

In my car, on the front passenger seat, I have today's *Cape Gazette*. I read about the new bills being introduced by the General Assembly to be passed into law in Delaware as a result of Bradley's actions. Already being referred to as the "Bradley Bills," they aim at improving oversight of the medical profession and strengthening patient protection in Delaware.

They're expected to fly through the house and senate a few weeks from now.

The new bills increase scrutiny physicians receive from the Board of Medical Practice while renewing their medical licenses and boost penalties for healthcare professionals who fail to live up to their legal responsibilities to report suspicious behavior by doctors. The new bills require additional child-abuse prevention training for medical professionals, law enforcement officers and prosecutors. They will require a physician treating a person 15 years of age or younger to have another adult in the room when that child is disrobed or undergoing certain physical exams. Tougher penalties imposed on individuals who abuse a child and are in a position of trust or authority. These same bills increase the medical board's authority to crack down on unprofessional conduct, enhance its ability to work with law enforcement to protect public safety, and give police access to additional information about physicians under investigation.

I lean back in my seat and take a deep breath. It is raining now. The rain drops muddy the black and white checkers of the building in front of me. They blur together, black into white, into gray; rain slides down the windshield of my car. I think how hard it will be to gauge how Bradley has affected relationships between patients, mostly children and young adults, and their doctors. I also think that most who have read about the case will never again fully trust their doctors. The one person in whom we used to place our faith.

As I pull out of the old Baybees' parking lot, I notice a singular wild rose bush about six feet high by 3 ft. wide. It is overgrown, brownish, and appears almost dead like everything else in this God-forsaken place. After an hour I'd given up on finding one item that showed any sign of life here, one thing that showed me that something had survived. But one single rose flourishes at the top of one lone bush despite the decay that surrounds it. It is bright red, shiny and bristling with health.

Suppression

I am going to Bradley's evidentiary hearing. The hearing takes place during those last few white-hot days of August in 2010. It is 95 degrees and unbearably humid. I am nervous. It is my first time venturing into the real world of criminals instead of simply watching them on TV or reading about them. This is real. Parking the car, I wonder if Bradley will be in court, never really believing he will be.

But he is here. All eyes in the courtroom seem to jump at once. Dismay, disgust, maybe even shock, when Earl Bradley enters the courtroom. Surrounded by three large corrections officers he hobbles into court shackled by ankle and hand cuffs and takes his seat next to his defense team. I can't believe it. There is an audible rustling of voices in the courtroom. I am shocked by his appearance. In fact I wouldn't have recognized him had he not been wearing the gray DOC jumpsuit and had he not been surrounded by these huge, muscle-bound, uniformed officers. How ironic that DOC stands for Department of Corrections, when my brain first registers it as short for doctor, the corners of my mouth turning slightly upward.

I look at him again: Gone are the 220 pounds, replaced instead by a frail, rumpled, very thin image of the man he'd once been. He must have lost 60 pounds I think. There is no muscle – you can see the flab through his shirt. His hair is longer and still stringy, still dirty. He still squints through thick wire-rimmed glasses. All the fat of his face has sunk into his neck which is still covered by a more salt then peppered beard. He struggles to get to his seat. The officers still surround him, not out of fear that he will escape, I'm sure, but so that someone doesn't take a shot at him. This new Earl Bradley is even creepier than before.

My seat is perhaps twenty feet behind the man who'd committed these heinous crimes. The lead prosecutors, the defense, reporters whose names I know from both the *News Journal* and the *Gazette,* are here. A local artist, Abraxas, has been hired by the Journal to act as sketch artist. No photos allowed. Michael Lopardi from the local CBS station sits next to me. Another reporter from WMDT, the ABC affiliate, sits in the row just ahead of mine. It is all men, mostly young men, on the right side of the room, and me who sit behind Bradley. I not only feel out of place, I feel old.

On the left side of the courtroom sit ten maybe fifteen people. Some are representatives from the Attorney General's office. Some are from Child Protective Services, where I learn they had had some two hundred children receiving counseling. They seem to know each other and I wonder if any of them are parents of the victims. No, I think, because how could they contain themselves – how could they bear to look at him, to be in the same room as the man who'd done this? I find out later that some of them are, in fact, here.

I think I can smell Bradley's dirty hair. I have a keen sense of smell and the scent of dirty hair mixed with body odor is distinctive and most certainly, offensive. I cannot imagine it is coming from anyone else sitting near me.

The courtroom is the way I'd imagined it – small-ish, old, antique-looking with flowered, colonial-type curtains on the small two-paned windows. Everything in the room is wood, perhaps the original wood, over 200 years old. This is the county seat, after all.

Judge William Carpenter sits on a raised platform behind his massive courtroom desk with the prosecution and defense tables facing him. He looks down on us all. Five wooden benches on each side of the room. Like a small wedding chapel I think, it is quaint.

When the prosecution shows a still photograph of the room where Bradley took the children, it is my first real glimpse into the horror that was the doctor's 'prize room.' I look up, half standing, craning my neck to see this picture because I can't quite believe it is almost exactly as I'd imagined: Dreary, with toys not neatly stacked but strewn.

The brownish carpet appears not exactly brown but dirty. *Why is everything in his world so filthy?* I ask myself. And the couch, the infamous couch, was being identified by the officer on the stand as the exact couch where he'd first seen, in videos, Bradley touch a 3-month-old child. The officer on the stand reports that within 60 seconds after Bradley began to remove the child's diaper, and the child was screaming "Mommy, Mommy!" the officer closed the file immediately and requested a new search warrant for what he knew, now, to be a case of child exploitation or rape.

It is called an evidentiary hearing because the defense is challenging the 'probable cause' of the warrant as well as the search and seizure of key evidence which resulted in Bradley's arrest back in December.

The defense is challenging the warrant and the search of the buildings which led to the discovery of damaging files:

Those thumb drives which showed Bradley raping his victims.

His defense wants this evidence thrown out.

They say...because the checkerboard building in which the recordings were found was not covered by the search warrant and because the most damning videos were found in this specific building, this is the reason for the appeal. They call this doctrine the "fruit from the poisoned tree." In other words, that this case was 'tainted' from the very beginning. Or... so they say.

Much of Bradley's appeal is routed in long and involved legalities but briefly, it has to do with the fourth amendment to the United States Constitution and is the part of the Bill of Rights which 'guards against *unreasonable searches and seizures*, as well as requiring any warrant to be judicially sanctioned and supported by *probable cause.*' What Bradley's public defender is asserting is that the execution of the search warrant and what was subsequently seized was wrongfully obtained. Therefore, *this* fruit from the poisonous tree becomes tainted, thereby possibly negating the evidence that will be used to convict Bradley.

His defense claims that their client's Fourth Amendment rights were violated when police knowingly entered buildings on Bradley's business property, which were not *individually* listed in the search warrant. They say that police had no right to search Bradley's computers since Bradley supposedly did not store medical records electronically.

I am aghast to think there is even a possibility that the eventual appeal might be heard, let alone that that it could generate a new trial or God forbid, that it could negate the fact that Bradley *is* guilty. How can this be, I ask? I cannot comprehend this way of thinking. When the hard evidence is staring you in the face, how can a lawyer…. how can anyone look for reasons or excuses to get a man like Bradley, declared 'not guilty?' *Why?* So his lawyer wins a case? So he gets an insane pedophile put back on the streets? I don't care about *his* supposed rights when the evidence is so startling. So obviously true. How much more trusted could the evidence be than his taking video by his own hand that shows the rape of young children? The whole thing is frustratingly infuriating. I try to remember I'm still in court reminding myself that my face is probably contorted in anger and confusion.

The moment comes in the hearing when I hope that Judge Carpenter decides *not* to suppress or 'throw out' the video evidence. It is at the crux of what the defense is challenging – the actual search warrant *execution*. My stomach is churning. Bent over, head down, I hit my fist into my other hand as the defense tries to discredit Detective Spillan. And I think, *Please God, don't let the Judge suppress this evidence.*

Would the judge then have to turn to the parents and the children as witnesses?

Wouldn't this then delay the case for many more months?

Wouldn't the suppression of this evidence infuriate the parents and make yet one more mockery of our justice system?

Months later we will learn the evidence shall *not* be suppressed.

It is lunch break "All rise!" Commands a court officer. As Bradley stands and waits for his escorts, he scans the room. His eyes land on mine and he stares directly into my eyes. I avert my gaze. I cannot bear his eyes looking into mine.

The Drive Home

On my drive home I am stopped at the red light on Rt. 9 and Coastal Highway/Route 1 just minutes from home. My mind wanders again to what his first night back in jail will be like after he'd felt the sunshine on his back, smelled the onions from the deli next door and heard the sounds of freedom: Horns honking on Main Street, lovers laughing as they walk by the back side of the courthouse, the smell of corned beef from the same deli. Simple, everyday sounds and smells.

That night, I imagine most everyone is asleep but him. It is 2:15 and he is still wired from his day in court. Does he think: Sometimes it seems as if it never happened. That he'd never put his hand down that first baby's diaper. That he hadn't used a hidden camera in an ordinary pen to capture the child's image. That he hadn't moved to Lewes, that he hadn't gone mad to rape all those children. Those images might scramble through his brain now.

They aren't in order.

They aren't in sync.

Maybe, it's as if it happened to someone else's life. As if his own father or his uncle or *someone*... hadn't abused him. As if his mother hadn't deserted him in both life and death; as if he'd never destroyed so many lives, including his own. If only there'd been someone early on to unscramble his brain; if only they'd seen the warning signs. If only they could have stopped it before it began, he wouldn't now be thinking this must have happened to another doctor, in another small town; someone else's heinous crimes.

Flying

I begin to wonder what my life will be like without him. What will I think of and what will I write about? Who will occupy that brain space where he resides? Who will I hate? He is a part of almost every waking moment now. All the

Meg Ellacott

time I ask myself questions like *what does he have to look forward to? What is he doing right now? What did he have for lunch? Does anyone visit him, talk to him?*

    I think about a future without Bradley in it as I drive to the Philadelphia Airport for a business trip to Las Vegas. *I Believe I can Fly* by R. Kelly plays on the radio. I think it is one of the most beautiful, inspiring, yet sad songs I know. Sad and beautiful don't seem like they belong with each other but I think about other sad, yet exquisite things in this world: baby sea turtles racing for the water's edge in time to be their predator's prey; being in love and having your heart broken. This obsession with Bradley tumbles through me as it has so many times before. I wish I could speak with him or someone close to him so I might begin to understand.

    I am nearing Dover and its air force base which is off to the right side of Route One. I marvel at the giant transport planes, the C-130s that fly to the Middle East and, each time I pass by, I think that these are the ones that bring back our dead or wounded from war.

    Suddenly I hear the roar of engines and one is on final approach from the West. An enormous shadow passes overhead. It grows in size, its shadow ripples and floods outward echoing the doom and tragedy it carries. My stomach churns. How long will the families wait until their children's or father's or brother's bodies are brought home to them? How many are in just one of these huge aircraft that passes overhead? I watch until it re-appears in my rearview mirror. It flares, flaps lowered, and is about to land. I think of the sadness within, the beauty within, and

143

then the darkness again. And this brings me back to thoughts of Bradley and the kids he hurt.

Who would I be once this story is over? Will I be any different? Where will I be in my head, once he no longer lives there?

The clouds are beginning to break now, the sun peeks through so there is dark and light simultaneously. I slip on my prescription grey-tinted sunglasses.

Somewhere between the longing for my old life, and some fear of going forward, lies acceptance: An acceptance that at some point his story and my search for answers will end. What is this fear I wonder? I find I have trouble answering this question: But then it comes – it is a fear, an uneasiness, of wanting more from Bradley. To get more direct answers from *him*. This reminds me of Truman Capote and *In Cold Blood* when he meets with his subjects, the killers of the Clutter family, and finds he feels compassion for them. A strange friendship begins. But Capote pulls away because it consumes him, because he does feel compassion for a killer and because it is all just too harsh to live with. He could not fathom that he became involved in a friendship that bordered on some kind of bizarre love with a murderer. Is this even akin to something I feel for Bradley? No, it is certainly not some kind of love or friendship but it is some kind of weird obsession, I think. My other fear is something I've felt almost always:

"Be careful what you wish for." I wanted to write. I longed to find a story to write about. And then I found one. And now I am hooked on this story like a junkie gets hooked on heroin. I need more.

How, I ask myself, can I get through to Bradley? How can I understand more? How can I bring him in to my confidence? Again, I whisper to myself "Be careful what you wish for."

A Letter

A towering black idea of a letter comes to mind – *one that is hand-written*. What if I could get to him by writing a letter in long hand? A real letter. I fixate on the word, lost in thought, the Dover Air Force base is behind me now. When was the last time I'd written in long-hand, a real letter? Who did I send it to? That pain-staking effort of putting pen to paper versus typing 90 words a minute and firing off a quick email. I can't believe I cannot remember the last time I wrote a letter. Was it a thank you letter some three years ago sent to a friend because of an unexpected gift? A business note asking someone to sign something? Instructions to send the check straight to the credit card company? It saddens me that I haven't written any long-hand letters that are more personal or more meaningful.

It is sadder to me still that I am thinking of writing a letter to a monster.

I find myself nearing Wilmington. Lost in thought, I hadn't even noticed the towns of Dover or Smyrna or Bear fly by – and normally I search the horizon at the Smyrna exit off Route 1 for a glimpse of the James T. Vaughn Correctional facility.

Where Bradley is housed.

If I write to him, will they intercept and preview my letter? I wonder. Are his letters even delivered to him or are they remanded first to his public defender? It is my understanding after talking about this with a friend who majored in criminal justice, that inmates do lose some rights prior to the court's final judgment. Their lawyer is usually privy to what the inmate can and can't respond to (she can't order but she can advise for the good of the case and her client). Might my letter simply be returned to me without being opened at all, marked "Return to Sender"

as if *he* doesn't exist at all?

DOC

I Google Department of Corrections and 'mail to inmates' and the only thing I can find is instructions on how to write to them...and a warning: "We urge the public to be cautious before establishing social relationships with offenders." The warning in itself, is enough to stop me. Bright red flags are waving again.

I am back home from my business trip to Las Vegas. Early morning clouds have dissipated giving rise to the warmth of the sun's golden rays. Settled back in my library, I wonder: What in the *hell* would I say in that letter? That I didn't want to talk about the case – I know I can't. I wouldn't ask questions about legalities but what I do want to know is – What is he feeling? What does this, his life as it is now, do to someone? Twenty-three hours alone in a jail cell. Who has he become? Actually, I'd like him to do all the talking. I wouldn't even have to ask him questions in my letters. He could just talk to me as if I were his shrink, his social worker...a friend?

The pit in my stomach is back. I think hard about this. How could I befriend a sex offender and worse, one that had hurt so many children right there at his pretend medical practice? I am reminded again of Truman Capote and *In Cold Blood*– his battle between befriending a murderer and simply writing about one and how doing so almost ruined his life. Could I really remain impartial or fair-minded?

In the end, I think I would fail at trying to do so.

Now I'm taken aback thinking how dare I compare what I am doing to what Truman Capote wrote about the Clutter Family; his compassion for Perry and Dick, his breathtaking description of the tiny town of Olathe, Kansas, his chilling descriptions of the murders. How dare I? And then, how alien it all must have been to him; how alien this is to me. And yet, like Capote, I am driven.

I honestly don't know if I can do it – i.e., sound genuine while trying to elicit a response. But I'll never know unless I try.

"Easy does it," I say to myself again. "Be careful what you wish for."

Evil

I heard this quote on the TV show Criminal Minds a while back: "Evil is always unspectacular and always human. It shares our bed and eats at our table."

It ricochets through my brain. I can't shake it. Sixteen words that describe precisely how evil exists in our everyday lives, and how mostly, we are unaware of it.

I've been watching a marathon of *The First 48*, a TV show about murder and mystery and the homicide detectives who solve these cases. Addicted to this show for months now, I often write about Bradley with true crime blaring in the background. It keeps me in the mood to write about criminal behavior. *The First 48* is about those critical hours at the start of a homicide investigation when a detective's chance of solving a murder is cut in half if he doesn't get a lead in those first two days.

On the TV, two kids find a body slumped over a swing in a park on the south side of Memphis, Tennessee. The victim has been shot in the back with a Colt 45. Homicide detective Tony Mullins, a sixteen-year police sergeant, is called to the scene.

The show's music unnerves me. I wonder how the clues will develop and which of those clues will bring the killers to justice. Mullins is the epitome of that veteran homicide cop: The proverbial beer gut, balding, hard, raw, but I sense a heart that is kind. I am unexpectedly attracted to the sweetness in this tough guy.

As I watch the show, I begin my own online research with www.ask.com, a site where you can ask any question and ask.com brings up tons of websites in response, questions from how many feet are in an acre to what is the time in Italy when it's 5pm in New York to what is the difference between a sociopath and psychopath? And that is my question today.

240 links pop up.

"You've got to be kidding," I say out loud. This statement is followed by a large, sucking sigh. Where do I even start? I stare at the list. Some are less interesting such as *Recognize a Psychopath, answers.yahoo.com* or *www.lovefraud.com*. On another site you can take a test to determine if you are a sociopath. Before I take the test, I notice there are several links beginning with "Start Online Dating Today." Does the website weed out the sociopaths for you, before you go out with one of these guys? I realize, of course, these are advertisers' links but this is what gets confusing – what is real and what is not? Who would click through to a dating site when they're researching psychopaths?

On www.AskDrRobert.com I read that Dr. Robert, a psychotherapist, says that there really is no difference between psychopaths and sociopaths. Other experts agree. For both you'd ask the following questions: "Is he/she unable to form any kind of emotional bond with another person? Does he or she seem to be *always* without empathy for others, even their own family?

Next Dr. Robert answers a question from a woman who is afraid she is living with a sociopath. Her boyfriend apparently makes her feel as though *she* is the crazy one. Dr. Robert has more questions for her: Does he do things that seem beyond comprehension? And then carry on as if those actions made no difference? Is he in trouble with the law and other authorities? Does he like dangerous, outrageous or socially/sexually unacceptable activities that provide a thrill?"

My mind wanders back to something else I'd read in *The Sociopath Next Door* which said "one in twenty-five people, or 4 percent of the population, have this condition of lacking conscience and guilt." Guiltlessness is, in fact, the first personality disorder to be recognized by psychiatry. Other terms for sociopathic behaviors that have been used over the past century include *manic sans delire*, moral insanity and moral imbecility. I remember that the book also alluded to the fact that sociopaths have an uncanny ability to steamroll over either individuals or groups of people who are highly dependent and voiceless. Of course, this is exactly what Earl Bradley did.

There's a good deal of psychological babble on the other sites I skim through - narcissistic personality disorder, borderline personality disorder, antisocial personality disorder - and my head begins to swim. I wish I'd paid more attention to my Abnormal Psych class in college. Of course, some of these behaviors hadn't even been discovered when I went to college.

Part of our grade in Abnormal Psych meant working for the State Mental facility, in Sunbury, Pennsylvania. It was one of the worst three months of my life. I dreaded going to the hospital to work with my assigned patient who was schizophrenic. The smell of urine, the stench of my patient, the ancient, dilapidated building and the screams of what sounded like tortured animals frightened me terribly. I almost dropped the class but ended up seeing it through. My patient and I played checkers. I took notes on his behavior. That was pretty much it.

I slip in and out of ten, twenty, sites and end up back at Dr. Robert. Apparently the question of the difference between a psychopath and sociopath has been argued for years amongst professionals in the psychiatric field. The question being "*Is* there a difference between the two?"

Some define a sociopath very simply as someone incapable of feeling guilt whereas a psychopath has more psychological pathology or mental illness than just the absence of guilt.

But why do the labels matter, I wonder. Earl Bradley is a psychotic sociopath and a raging pedophile. Why isn't this enough for me? Is it because I still feel I haven't defined him yet? And why is it important to me to do so? I go skating through the websites again – that's what it feels like to me – like I'm flying with sudden jerky stops and starts, reading intros on every site until I dig my heel into the ice for a sudden stop…read, read and then race on to the next one.

I keep reading and learn that a sociopath is a much older term. In fact one site says "most uninformed people try to draw a distinction between the two, assuming a psychopath is much 'worse' than a sociopath." But this, it says, "is incorrect." "The two terms mean exactly the same thing." Both terms simply refer to the fact that the affected person is "incapable of feelings of guilt." So why am I so dead set on finding the difference?

Dr. Robert then says that "more 'uninformed' people try to argue that all psychopaths or sociopaths are somehow evil-intentioned, malevolent, or maleficent. He says that "*Intention*, evil or otherwise, is not what defines the psychopath. Nor is an evil *deed* or a despicable *action* a test for psychopath. Psychopathy involves one, and *only* one, criterion: *is the person psychologically capable of feeling guilty?*" The internet is starting to wear me down now.

Even though the room is dark, I can tell the sun is low on the horizon, casting a deep amber hue in the bedroom. It has become warmer in my room as the day reaches into night. Dr. Robert's website mentions 'evil' in one of his paragraphs. And evil is a running theme here, isn't it? Where does evil come from? Can we be born evil? Is evil a religious concept, a philosophical term, sociological or yet one more psychological term? *Evil*. I fall back to that tantalizing quote that brought me here in the first place: Evil, in fact, *is* human. It *is* always unspectacular and it *does* share our lives.

Earl

I take a break, set the computer aside and step outside for a while. The month has secretly slipped from August to September. I sit at the little brown metal table on my deck with its lime green chairs and prop my feet on the side rail of the hot tub. Early evening and the clouds are brilliant in swirls of red, orange, deep blues and grey.

Can Bradley see this incredible sky-scape from his barred window?

I decide to scrap much of what I'd written on psycho vs. sociopath. As I think back to what I'd already written, the words just blur into one another. Only the word *evil* consumes me.

Later, as the sky turns dark I am back at the computer. I turn on the TV once again, this time to WBOC News where I learn that Hurricane Earl is heading up the east coast. Yes, *Earl*. I think *of all the names they could have chosen....*

He just never goes away.

This hurricane appears dangerous with a possible direct hit to the Carolina's before it rides up the coast right through Rehoboth and Lewes. Earl, the fifth named storm of the 2010 hurricane season has maximum sustained winds of 145 mph. The news is over and I think how strange it is to learn about a storm named Earl and in the same broadcast I learn more about the hearing I'd just attended days before the Hurricane. Earl.

I am probably the only one in town to notice the irony, the ridiculous incongruity of it.

More Evil

Evil: There must be thousands of definitions, tests and hypotheses for the word evil. I need to narrow the search but after reading from just one site, which talks about drowning puppies, ways to kill and not get caught and suffering made simple I just want to quit and crawl under the covers.

I move on to another site. Samuel Butler describes evil this way: "It is like water. It abounds, is cheap, soon fouls but runs itself clear of taint." Another writer, St. Ambrose says "There is nothing evil save that which perverts the mind and shackles the conscience."

The poet Alain Badiou says that "Evil is the interruption of a truth by the pressure of particular or individual interests."

I stop to think about this last quote. I dissect it. I come to understand the larger picture of its meaning, about the interruption of truth...anyone's truth, which can be compromised if pressured by one's own selfish interests or obsessions

I read quickly now, and then more slowly, trying to soak it all in as I click through link after link. Overhead the fan whirs on high.

"Evil usually enters the world unrecognized by the people who open the door and let it in," I read. Most people who perpetrate evil do not see what they are doing as evil. It primarily exists in the eye of the beholder, especially in the eye of the victim. If there were no victims, there would be no evil. The words echo: *If there were no victims, there would be no evil.* It is so obvious, yet so profound.

"No evil dooms us hopelessly except the evil we love, and desire to continue in, and make no effort to escape from," George Eliot writes. I find this particular description of evil, bitter-sweet and strikingly touching. Why, I wonder.

I think about it in part, because I fear it describes a piece of me. I think there must be evil that dwells within me. How else to explain why I am so addicted to Bradley's story?

I find a quote which, perhaps, answers this question: "Evil is easy, and has infinite forms," by Blaise Pascal.

My eyelids are heavy, my eyes scratchy when my head hits the pillow. But I am not yet finished with evil. Not yet. My thoughts return to "the perpetrators of long time evil who require at least the passive cooperation of those who see it." I think about how most people undoubtedly prefer to believe that *they* would take a stand against evil if it were happening in their community. But it is easy to be virtuous in hypothetical situations. Most, I think, do not protest or try to stop evil. Would I? I'd like to believe I would but....

How do we understand this silence?

Dreams

Autumn of 2010 is grey and cold. October juxtaposes itself like a harsh wind against the warmest summer on record. There are no lazy ocean breezes, little vibrant color in the trees, smaller pumpkin harvests. This autumn takes these things and turns them icy before November has time to breathe. Before we have time to prepare ourselves for the unexpected depth to which this particular fall will take us. It is not the comforting, familiar autumn I'd come to expect. It tears through me like shredded lace.

It is one year this October that the hard evidence to arrest Bradley materialized. The point where a Mother and Father first realize their daughter had been molested by Bradley. The point where the final piece of the puzzle came together.

One year ago. I catch my breath. I can't believe it's been almost a year since 'Melissa' told her parents that Dr. Bradley had hurt her. It feels like only a few months ago I started writing about the case. About him. And it suddenly occurs to me that now, this fall, I'd missed the rebirth of spring and hadn't felt the warmth of this past summer - I was so busy reading and writing about the case.

Except for the searing heat, this is mostly all I remember about 2010.

On this autumnal night, the buzzing of the phone jerks me out of a dream. Before snatching the phone from the nightstand my eyes slide around the room, one that is filled with gleaming moonlight. I can see the outline of the flat screen TV, one of the dogs fast asleep next to the queen-sized bed and the green blinking clock light. 11:45 pm. My heart pounds from the shrill ring of the phone. I feel chilled from the sweat on my body. I am angry that someone is calling this late; fearful at the same time that it could be an emergency. Suddenly, I realize I was dreaming about him.

The sheets feel damp, rumpled. Flustered and groggy I stretch out my arm and snatch the cordless phone from atop the night stand. The dream is still vivid in my mind. It plays out like a movie on the blank screen of my bedroom ceiling. Dropping my head back on the pillow with the wireless phone still pinned to my ear, my sister yaps about something I can't hear, nor do I want to. Something about a TV show….*America's Got Talent.* Since my sister is in the music business, she often calls at any time of the night, to talk about some singer or some emerging artist. My eyes are shut now. I am ready to hang up.

Trying to cling to this disappearing dream, I tell my sister I will call her tomorrow. I close the phone, slowly resting it, and my hand, on my chest. I feel hot and sweaty and can't decide if it is because Maggie has jumped on the bed and has snuggled too close to my legs or because of this fitful dream. And then it hits me:

The force of what I dreamed jars through my bones. The fragmented images fire off in my brain. The pictures are swirling inside but I remember – his filthy, gigantic hands on *me* – the dirty room, assaulting *me,* trying to rape *me.*

My eyes follow the motion of the fan above the bed. I can hear it's gentle whirring as the blades swing round and around. He was wearing those stained corn-flower blue scrubs; he grits his teeth – explosive anger – pulled my hair. My arms are pinned at my sides. Had I been on the floor in the dream? Or on that dark grey couch I'd seen in the picture at the court hearing? - The same couch where he....

The images began to fade. I don't want to remember this, I think. But I can still feel the nubbly, scratchy texture of the couch against my skin. That couch. The smell of urine mixed with dirt.

"I've got you, you bitch," Bradley kept whispering in my ear.

The dream fades until it vanishes to black.

Shaken, I wrap my arms around myself and turn to face Maggie. She stirs and crawls up to my face, sensing I'm awake. Sensing I'm upset. She sniffs my face, then my ears and rests her head on my elbow. She knows. She can feel my fear or my sadness. I am not sure which.

I reach out to stroke her sweet face. My eyes are shut tight. Achy butterflies float through my stomach. It is almost midnight.

Depression or heartache or fear wash through me.

I haven't cried since, since....when? Since before I started writing about Bradley? But the tears come tonight. I lean to the bottom of the bed and pull up the throw blanket and pull it tight under my chin. My grief seems unstoppable, the tears keep streaming. After a few minutes they suddenly stop. "It was just a dream," I keep repeating. "It was just a dream."

Sleepy now I think of him, not the dream. I roll over placing the phone into its cradle on the nightstand and wish I could tell him: Everywhere I look, I see you. After eight months, you wash through me like dust rolling through a desert storm. Like the dying corn husks in the field behind my house. I can hear you as their harsh, burnt leaves rustle in the autumn wind. You are everywhere but mostly you are in my mind, always, as I wrestle for ways to describe the how and why of what you did. Almost daily now, I yearn for the chosen, reassuringly familiar life I used to live. Before you.

Warning

Tennessee Williams said "We are all of us sentenced to solitary confinement in our own skins, for life."

Imagine. This is Earl Bradley – sentenced to solitary confinement in his own skin, for life.

Imagine, for I cannot – attempting to live a life knowing what he, himself did. None of us will know until the trial what exactly made Earl Bradley into the man he was. Even then, what happened and why may always remain a mystery. What *is* known is that he suffered from extreme depression, drug abuse and a type of disorder or mental illness. It is believed he self-medicated with prescription drugs (possibly narcotics and perhaps abusing alcohol as well) while simultaneously weaning himself off the prescribed meds for a reported bi-polar disorder. His father was accused of molesting children. His uncle was actually charged with sexually exploiting children. Is it then safe to assume Bradley, somewhere along the way was himself, sexually abused? Perhaps violently?

Maybe there are some people who should just come with warning labels, I often think. Maybe Bradley suffered a psychotic break as a young man or maybe this break could have propelled itself when his wife left him or his family started to unravel back in the late 1990s. It is an understatement to say he was deeply troubled. Perhaps as a child he suffered from some kind of anxiety or disassociative disorder or other type of psychosis. If so he lived in a world of uncontrollable behaviors, never knowing what would come next. But it is no storybook tale when mental illness happens in real life. It can be a world of explosive behavior and imaginary images; or a world where he might have battled invisible phantoms or major mood swings both depressive and manic, like living with a bomb ready to detonate. Or maybe, somewhere on his way through childhood, he simply missed a connection or two. For reasons still a mystery, his once happy life turned into a nightmare somewhere along the way.

Pedophile Profile

Sexual abuse appears to be a common thread in addictive behavior. The trauma of the abuse often leads to severe addictions. In part because 'trauma' often shatters the way the brain regulates itself. So the longer someone doesn't deal with, or recover from, trauma, the worse the 'regulation' or coping methods become. In other words "We are only as sick as our secrets."

It seems then, that for eleven years after Bradley's wife left him and prior to his arrest, he lived in some kind of 'altered' state. With the exception of his extreme rage and violence, he did display almost every characteristic of the 'typical' pedophile profile.

Child predators are usually single males over the age of 30; they have few friends their own age; there may be time gaps in employment – for questionable reasons. (The time gap I found in Bradley's life was just after college when not much is known about him except that he drove a cab.) Predators are often fascinated with children and child-like activities. They often refer to children in pure or angelic terms, using words like innocent, heavenly, divine. Bradley often referred to his little patients as 'angels.'

A pedophile's hobbies are child-like such as collecting popular and expensive toys, keeping exotic pets or building plane and car models. All around Bradley's medical practice were strewn carnival rides, Big-Wheels, expensive dolls and other play things. Even more chilling is that pedophiles often change their living arrangements or have a special room which is decorated in child-like décor and appeals to the children he is trying to entice. The prize room, the Disney-themed exam rooms, popsicles and bowls of candies roar into my brain.

Sadly predators often seek out shy, handicapped, and withdrawn children or those who come from troubled or under-privileged homes. I think of the children Bradley molested who were autistic or developmentally delayed or from lower income families. He then showered them with attention, gifts and toys.

Additionally I'd read there are categories of pedophiles: Situational and preferential: Situational: rarely seeks out their victim but takes advantage of the situation when presented with it. Preferential (Bradley): Actively seeks out and targets by age group, hair color, gender and seeks jobs that give them as much access to children as possible.

He was a pediatrician.

They were all young girls except one boy.

If any parent, any one, had read this list of characteristics before entering Baybees Pediatrics, they would not have gone near Dr. Bradley. He fit not one, not two of the traits on this list, but every one of them.

Then there were other doctors, registered nurses, other medical professionals who put their kids in his care. They thought he was a talented doctor, with a unique gift for relating to children. A mother of a 7-year-old, who chose Bradley based on the recommendation of nurses at the hospital the day her daughter was born said, "He didn't talk well with parents but with kids he was the best she'd ever seen." When she reflects on her decision, she says "I look back now and realize that was the day I could have changed a lot of things."

The doctor struck others as "accommodating and competent." He frequently met them at off-hours and sometimes didn't charge for minor consultations. Building trust, overly caring, priming or grooming his target, this is what predators do.

I found more warning signs: If an adult pays more attention to children than he does to adults, this can be a red flag. They build trust children often crave and once given the attention, the pedophile takes advantage of that trust. Abusers often fool themselves into thinking the child wants the affection. Is this what Bradley thought? I wondered. That he was giving an unloved child much-needed care or attention?

I learned too that if a child worships an adult (a doctor for instance) or looks up to him, these children often become the perfect target for a pedophile. Pedophiles sometimes give the child back or foot-rubs so the child gets used to someone having their hands on him or her. Many times, this helps prime the child for intimacy. Once the pedophile engages with his victim, it makes the predator feel powerful. And abusers are truthfully, and unbelievably, unaware of the damage they have done, often only becoming aware of their damaging actions once, and if, they get help. I do not feel this to be the case with Earl Bradley because he was a sociopath, never feeling he needed help, never showing remorse for what he'd done. Ever. Anger once again oozes through me when I think of just how much damage he caused.

I read in Secret Survivors by Susan Blume that approximately one in seven boys and one in four girls in the United States today has been sexually molested as a child. I read in that same book that pedophiles will do anything to protect their world of sexual intimacy with 'their' children. In fact one story currently circulating tells of the sadistic depths to which Bradley went to protect that world.

A parent, a mother, came to Bradley with her daughter. She said she was nervous, and confused. There seemed to be some redness and discomfort in the area of her daughter's vagina. The doctor, feigning concern, asked her to wait outside the exam room while he phoned Child Protective Services and asked them to 'look into this case,' implying the mother or her husband could have abused their own daughter. He closed the exam room door, forcing the mother to wait. In fact, Bradley had been the one who had molested their daughter.

The woman was of illegal U.S. status, Hispanic in origin and was therefore easily intimidated. Uncertain and fearful, she'd stood outside the exam room door pleading with the doctor not to call child advocacy. During those few minutes she waited on the other side of the closed door, never having suspected him in the first place, she screamed "I was wrong to bring this up – Just give me back my daughter." Apparently during those few minutes, Bradley had enough time to again sexually molest her child, all the while torturing the young mother.

Notorious

The charges against Bradley rank him among other notorious medical professionals who throughout history have done great harm under the guise of medicine. The other day in my unending search for Bradley clues, I found him online, ranked among other "most criminally insane real world medical professionals." On one Science and Technology website Bradley is ranked toward the top alongside Cecil Jacobson, who was found guilty of impregnating patients by inseminating them with his own sperm. He was officially the father of eight children, but the estimated number is upwards of 75.

On the same website I find Dr. Harold "Frank" Shipman who in 1998 was convicted of murdering his patients by purposely overdosing them. Victims numbered upwards of

250 or more. Bradley is being compared to 'criminally insane medical professionals as far back as 1907 when Dr. Linda Burfield Hazzard who published Special Method of Forced Starvation, lured in unsuspecting patients with promises of fantastic health benefits. As Hazzard's methods caused her patients to grow weaker, she gradually convinced them to turn over their bank accounts and powers of attorney. Several died in her "care" as she became rich.

Noted German physician and SS Officer in the Auschwitz-Birkenau concentration camp during World War II, Dr. Josef Mengele is probably history's most notorious "Angel of Death." Mengele performed 'studies' on heredity by using the prisoners in the concentration camp as human guinea pigs. He showed a particular interest in studying twins, dwarfs and other people with physical abnormalities. The 'tests' Mengele conducted were unspeakably cruel, and included amputations, brutal "surgeries," shock treatments, and outright killing pairs of twins to study their postmortem anatomy in depth. He escaped after the war, and was hunted as a war criminal for the rest of his life – but he evaded capture, living in Brazil until his death in 1979.

Earl Bradley, being the most recent addition to this list, was ranked number two on this recording of twelve of the most diabolical medical criminals in history dating back to the beginning of the twentieth century.

Another Parent

I schedule a much needed manicure today. Amy would be my manicurist. I haven't seen her in a long time and we have a lot of catching up to do. She doesn't know I am working on the Bradley story so I fill her in. Talking long after my nail polish has dried, she tells me of a friend whose child had been repeatedly raped by Bradley. This woman was enmeshed in the evidence and witness gathering for the trial. Amy tells me how her friend's life had crumbled since being notified by police that her child was one of his victims. How there were images of her child being repeatedly abused by the doctor. They asked if she would come in to talk with authorities.

Amy tells me how the mother couldn't sleep, couldn't work, could barely function and would sometimes call Amy at 4:00 in the morning just to talk. Amy is a mother too. So Amy would wake at 4am, put on her coat, grab the leash and cell phone and while walking the dog in the dark, listen to her friend sob as dawn peeked over the horizon. How would her friend ever get past the guilt? How could she go on, knowing what she knew? How could she help her daughter? She is one of several, who would, eventually, move out of state.

She asked Amy, "Should I cooperate with police? Will my daughter remember the wounds inflicted by a doctor before she could even speak? Should I put her through all this when really, maybe, she'd never remember this as she grows up?" Amy just listened. The worst part was helping to get her friend through the guilt. No matter how many times she told this mother, "It's not your fault. You couldn't have known," it doesn't matter. She still feels horrible guilt and shame.

"In a way," Amy says, "it was almost cult-like the way his 'followers' believed in him, which made the betrayal that much worse." In fact, "It went beyond betrayal," Amy says. Her friend told her that while giving evidence and working with Biden's office, she heard that one of the doctors who had worked with Bradley, had actually said "Bradley is doing stuff he shouldn't be doing." This is the same pediatrician who called Bradley a pedophile *out loud.*

I still say he didn't know the extent to which Bradley had gone. How could he have? I don't believe that any doctor would knowingly hide a pedophile. Who *wouldn't* turn him in if they knew? But, he had a legal responsibility. As ordinary citizens we have a moral responsibility to blow the whistle on people we *think* could be hurting children. But the medical community has an absolute legal responsibility to bring such behavior to the Medical Board, law enforcement, CPS…anyone who could have taken action.

We both cry when we are through. Once again, the Bradley story has become very, very real to me.

Rapist

Bradley is a deviant sociopath. Combine this portrayal with bi-polar disorder as well as extreme depression, substance abuse and major childhood trauma and you have a serial rapist of the most violent kind. There is a history of child molestation in his family background. Yet another article in *The News Journal* reports that his father had a fascination with child pornography. These influences lead many to label

Bradley as mentally defective. Others call him delusional; still others deem him deranged.

WBOC, our local CBS affiliate channel, found lost footage in the station's archives of an interview with Earl Bradley from 2005; I watched this footage briefly in the Spring, but now watch it more carefully. I am still trying to find clues about the man behind the predator.

The news broadcaster introduces the segment by saying "Some of you might find this footage disturbing to watch in light of today's alleged crimes." It is. Disturbing.

He appears on my TV screen, this 6 foot, 220 pound bear of a man, in his every-day grimy blue scrubs. He cradles an infant's head in one hand, while the baby's body floats down his forearm. His hands appear extraordinarily large to me. They remind me of bear paws. It is my first careful look into Bradley's appearance, his demeanor and his office. Video from an innocent trip to the doctor one day, long ago.

As Bradley holds in one hand, the child who is wearing only a diaper, he strokes and palpitates him with the other, turning the child this way and that, apparently searching for rashes and skin infections. This is a story about the outbreak of hand, foot and mouth disease in Sussex County. A strip of Winnie the Pooh wallpaper peeks from behind the exam table.

The wallpaper and the doctor disturb me. I wonder how many times Bradley had violated a child while Disney characters danced in the background.

The doctor's hair is slicked with grease against his forehead as he squints, almost painfully, during the interview. I find out later that his eyesight was so poor that he sometimes wore two pairs of glasses at the same time. I focus in on those hands which appear, again, extraordinarily large on screen. He seems uncomfortable in front of the camera, shifting from one foot to the other, speaking quietly, almost in a whisper. I have to lean in to the TV to hear him. I know the doctor is innately shy, yet I see, what I think is pride in his squinty eyes. Is he proud the station has chosen him for this interview? Proud that, finally, he is getting the respect and notoriety he felt he rightfully deserved?

The one word that keeps filtering through my brain is 'disgusting,' mainly because of the way he looks, physically. His hair. His hair is not only dirty, it looks as though he'd cut it himself; a pageboy-type cut. It is filthy. Stains show on the blue scrubs. His graying beard appears unkempt. I'm appalled. How could so many patients have stayed with this man? I wonder how could so many patients have been this desperate? This fooled. The segment ends with several different shots of Bradley's hands: Touching a baby. Holding flu serum. In handcuffs.

Even though I briefly watched the footage months ago, I am more keenly aware now. I am shocked again listening to his voice. He is unbelievably soft spoken, so much so that he sounds like a woman.

Crossing Lines

Although I've learned about Bradley's childhood, I wonder again what could have led him to step over the line from miserable loner to prolific baby rapist. Is it a line someone crosses or does it happen gradually?

I learned a new term on *Criminal Minds*. *Anger excitation* which means the perpetrator becomes excited by the suffering of his victims. And by videotaping his attacks, he can relive the pleasure he's experienced with those victims again and again. What was it in his background that had reinforced his association between suffering and gratification? What happened to him? I keep thinking there must have been *something*...

Right from Wrong

I am almost ashamed at how much this information gathering thrills me. Why am I so thrilled by this case? Is this part of the evil within I thought of earlier? Is it the sensationalism of the case and the fact it happened just down the street? Is it some kind of illicit pleasure I too am deriving? I wonder again about why so many of us are vicariously thrilled by grisly horror stories. It is because we know that those stories are something that exist *outside* of us. Don't they?

I know or at least I think, that I am safely ensconced in my own highly developed conscience, my own sense of guilt, right from wrong. This keeps me safe. Or does it? Stephen King once said "We make up horrors to help us deal with the real thing." King also wrote "Monsters are real. They live inside us, and sometimes they win." As it was with Bradley, does a monster live somewhere inside me?

Psychopath

Where and when does normal behavior veer to not ordinary I wonder? When does checking and re-checking a locked door become a compulsion? When does counting the even numbers versus the odd become the norm and when does worrying that you might hurt someone by just thinking bad thoughts become obsessive compulsive? When does the need to protect become so compulsive that you destroy instead of defend? Somewhere along the way, Bradley's world became dangerously compulsive. We know he wasn't born like this. Or do we?

I watched another TV show a few nights ago called "Nighttime Prime – Secrets of Your Mind." It was a journey into the mind and heart of a psychopath. They asked the question "Are psychopaths wired differently than the rest of us?"

I learned that recent research suggests that psychopathy is evidenced in the brain and that those who end up raping or killing *can be* and *are* born to do so. Just as there is a genetic tendency toward addiction, so too, might some be born with 'neurological glitches" in their brains making them more prone to violence? Did Bradley get some kind of mental rush from raping small children? Like the rush one might get when addicted to cocaine or alcohol?

When I look at Bradley I see hate. I see fear and depression. He appears emotionless. Research shows that some people's brains have a structural deformity in the frontal part of the brain that controls emotion. People with this 'deformity' don't have normal feelings of revulsion and disgust and they typically have a callous disregard for human life. A murderer studied on *Secrets of the Mind* who bludgeoned his victims to death speaks of his acts as you'd expect a psychopath to do. No guilt, no remorse, no conscience: Quite simply, 'it was what it was.' The notorious killer, Tommy Lynn Sells, says on this show he was after the 'drug.' His drug: the addiction to taking a life. A serial rapist, like a killer, in his first rape usually experiences a type of euphoria which he continues to chase but usually is unable to achieve again.

When they scanned and analyzed Sells' brain, they found this was a brain vulnerable to violence. He had very low activity in his prefrontal cortex. In images of a normal brain, this area is brighter in color – deep blues, greens and reds; in the front of the murderer's brain, that same region is dark, cold and empty showing only in tones of black and gray.

If we could only see inside Bradley's brain.

Would his defense ever take a CT scan of his brain? What would be found? Who would have been the role of genetic inheritance in Bradley's criminal behavior? But genetically influenced behavior is a new field and it is a relatively new legal tactic called Neurolaw, meaning that brain imaging can be used to attempt to exonerate psychopaths who would otherwise be found guilty and sent to jail. Has this new legal tactic matured enough to be allowed or admitted into court?

The whole notion unsettles me. Should society be fearful of neurolaw? Isn't this just one more law developed to help criminals escape prosecution? At society's expense? So far, this tact has been used in some criminal cases to spare monstrous criminals from the death penalty. *Is this just an excuse? A sophisticated way of excusing violent behavior?* I ask myself. God forbid they do decide to use this defense in Bradley's case. Could Bradley's dysfunctional brain from birth, have played a role in the rape of all those children?

How could I have known when I first started writing about this that there are some wounds that are worse than fatal.

That there are some victim's wounds the law cannot fully understand nor can it fix.

Part IV: Winter 2010-2011

The Winds of Delaware bellow and blow gusting up to 30 knots today.

The shingles on my house shutter. The windows rattle.

It is December 2011. It is the anniversary of his arrest two years ago today.

And this is fitting, for when I think of him I think of how the winds whip the air into frenzy here at the beach.

And I think of how frenzied his violence was toward the children.

He came to our shores, abruptly, unexpectedly, like a fierce wind does when it strikes here at the beach.

And then he - And then the wind - is gone, as suddenly as it appeared.

The winds mysteriously descend upon us, as he did.

It sucks away our breath, as he did.

Then too, it washes through us, shaking us into understanding - as he did when we learned a child predator lived in our midst;

And <u>how</u> it can happen here; and <u>how</u> it can happen anywhere?

Sometimes the winds here in Delaware turn cold, harsh and brutal.

This doctor. This monster, was much, much worse:
quite severely,
quite utterly,

quite intolerably, much worse than the winds of Delaware.

A Look Back at 2010

I focus again on the pile of newspapers and magazines on my desk but find myself thinking of the year in general, not just of Earl Bradley. It was a year when we lost *Leave It to Beaver's mom*, Barbara Billingsly; major movie mogul Tony Curtis and actress, Lynn Redgrave; Elizabeth Edwards, someone I'd come to care about and highly respect as a writer; someone who had written about Rehoboth Beach in her memoir and then, would die of cancer. This was the year when 33 Chilean Miners were trapped and then rescued after 69 days in the cold and dark. They too must have felt like they were being smothered.

Like the snow smothered our beach towns last year.

Like Bradley smothered his victims.

2010 was the year of major disasters, both natural and manmade: the awful BP oil spill; the devastating Haiti Earthquake. I can't help but see similarities, this time, between the spill, the trapped minors and Bradley. How many kids had Bradley trapped? And the thick, disgusting oil slick - 206 million gallons of it, almost 20 times the Exxon Valdez spill, floating freely, killing 6,000 birds, 600 sea turtles and 100 dolphins and other sea mammals. Monstrous numbers. Like the ones connected to Bradley: Over 500 charges against 127 children. Over 500.

2010 was the year when Tiger Woods, one of the best golf pro of all time would betray his family again and again; it was a time of Obama Healthcare which would spur months of political debate and potential repeal by Republicans. And it was a year in the technology sector where the iPad® would rule – the iPad, as strange as science-fiction but real - changing the way we live, even the way we do business at the touch of a button. A year of joy when a young prince would ask a mere commoner to wed, reminding most baby boomers of the Prince's long-deceased mother, Princess Diana. 2010 was a time of survival too when an icon entertainer, Michael Douglas would reveal he had throat cancer and battle it to emerge victorious just days before I write this.

One of the last reports of the year occurred just before Christmas when Mark Madoff, son of reviled liar and Wall Street embezzler, Bernie Madoff, killed himself while his baby son slept in the room next door. Bernie Madoff. A father. A monster. Someone who'd defrauded hundreds of his friends and family members out of $65 million in stock market scams. I recall Madoff's crimes and again wonder about Bradley's victims and his own four children. Had his son ever considered the same thing? Had shame ever made him feel so desperate, that he too thought about killing himself because *his* father was Earl Bradley? Mark Madoff killed himself on the very day of his father's arrest, two years earlier.

Anniversary

It snowed today, one year to the day of his arrest. A day of gloom; a grim reminder of what happened December 16 2009. I stand outside on my covered deck looking between the fence and the mud-filled fields out back. The sky is slate gray, agitated; a raw dampness to the air. Throughout much of the day I watch the snow fall, this drenching of cold confetti as it plummets to the ground. The evergreens became laden with snow like soaked cotton balls - giant fir trees droop their strong branches. Later today, when it stops and the sun warms the air, the snow will start to melt as thoughts of Bradley dissipate with it.

Everything is gray and flat outside my window as I watch the smothering snow and think back to the time of his arrest. Even then I felt as if something as cold and barren as this snowstorm had come to our beach town. For months afterward I wondered if it was only me: Was I the only one who felt this <u>level</u> of disappointment and betrayal because of what he'd done? I knew later that, most certainly, I was not alone.

I also know that tragedies like this don't always happen elsewhere. Sometimes they come right to your front door. We no longer lived in a time where parents said "don't talk to strangers" because the predator's playground had extended beyond the schoolyard, beyond the playgrounds. Those days had disappeared – because 90% of sexually abused children <u>know</u> the person who molested them. One year later, I ask myself *what else I had learned*.

I have learned that one in four girls is sexually abused each year and one in six or seven boys. I've learned that twenty percent of all children receive unwanted sexual messages and that seventy-five percent of those children do *not* tell their parents. And I know that each year there are 400,000 new victims of sexual assault. That here in the small state of Delaware there are 2,700 registered sex offenders. Even now, I struggle to wrap my head around these simple numbers when I remember another statistic about child molesters: seventy-six percent of serial rapists claim they were molested as children. I am suspicious of this. I would think it closer to ninety percent – that perhaps those pedophiles studied did not want to report their own abuse. Nonetheless, the incidence of abused children who then go on to molest children as adults is numbing. It is clear I know more about child sexual abuse than I ever wanted to. And I wish I didn't.

I pull my seashell-designed blanket up around my shoulders thinking of the parents again. They are usually my last thought when I am thinking or writing about Bradley – my mind automatically turning to their sorrow. Then I think that probably many of them may never know if Bradley harmed their child. What must this last year have been like for them? Living with the *hope* that Bradley had not touched *their* child. I imagine even their hope must feel treacherous. Hoping - Were their kids seen in any of the mounds of video tape police confiscated? And even if their children were not in Bradley's video footage, what does this mean? It just means that he didn't video what he *might* have done to them. The parents, the families remain suspended.

I believe that now, a year later, my sadness for the families has leveled off somewhat or I've simply gotten used to it being a part of my life. Or that my life, with him in it, has taken on a kind of normalcy now, one that is almost companionable. I've written about him for so long his story has become a part me. And I am almost comforted by this ugly story rather than tortured by it. But what does that mean? Have I turned some corner? Have I lost my ability to feel, to revel in rage or delve into deep, deep sadness?

Up until December 16, 2009 I could have told you what I believed in with relative ease.

I believed in respect and love for myself and others.

I believed in family and friendship.

I believed in confidence and strength to keep putting one foot in front of the other no matter what.

I believed in faith, honor, responsibility and trust – not necessarily in that order.

Trust.

That word now sticks in my throat. It has been compromised.

Hadn't I always believed that you could trust, without restraint, certain people in this world? Your brother, your sister, parents, teachers, spiritual leaders - your doctors? And despite the daily news about sadness and duplicity, despite 9/11 and child rape in the church, and parents murdering their own children, I still, at age 58, believed that people were mostly good – I never knew, until a year ago, that sociopaths walked beside us. I never knew much about sociopaths at all.

What I Know

Now I believe that there really are, plain and simple, *evil* people not only out there – but here, right here in our towns, our neighborhoods, our communities. I know that approximately one in twenty five people is a sociopath; that they could be someone I know, work with, go to writing class with. It could be Georgia, the odd one in class; or Barry, my best guy friend and neighbor. These people might lack the most meaningful of all characteristics, one that divides the human species from all others - the presence or absence of conscience – sometimes referred to as the seventh sense. There is, quite simply, a black hole where the conscience should be. And so I know that by far, Bradley's most impressive talent was his ability to conceal from nearly everyone the true emptiness of his heart. And to command the passive silence of his prey.

I now know that sociopaths don't necessarily look like Charles Manson – the murderer with the wild, crazed look in his eyes. They look like us. Ordinary, unassuming. I now know to <u>always</u> listen to my instincts. Had more listened to the voices in their heads, Bradley most probably would have been caught earlier.

I now know to watch out for liars, for deceit is the linchpin of conscienceless behavior.

Today I question authority more so, even when everyone around me has stopped questioning it. I read that at least six out of ten people will blindly obey an official-looking authority. Like Bradley in his scrubs or white doctor's coat.

I've also learned to become more suspect of flattery – especially when it is extreme or unnatural. Counterfeit charm usually means someone is trying to manipulate me. Spotting the false charm though, is the trick.

I now admit I've always had a tendency to pity too easily.

To feel sorry for certain people, to give too much, to help too easily.

But pity should be reserved for innocent people. For those in genuine pain or for those who have fallen on tough times. But I used to also pity even those who consistently hurt me, who had campaigned for my sympathy. This is something that has changed, for sociopaths live for your pity. Once they've got it, they've got you.

I've finally acquiesced that I can't redeem the unredeemable. How many times had I tried to *save* someone who never wanted to be saved? I now know the disappointing lesson that no matter how good my intention, I can't control or change the character of someone else. I'd learned, finally that I could only help those who wanted it and to help only when it doesn't damage me.

I was thinking this as I walk the dogs. I am almost running them home now, it is so cold. All around me, icy white: The dirt-white of chimney smoke, my own opaque breath as I trudge home, the smell of new snow and icicles already forming on roof overhangs. The only thing I can hear above the wind that whips my face is my own feet and the dogs crunching through the snow. I ask myself what else I've stopped believing in or what else I've learned a year after his arrest?

I have learned more about crime victims.

Mostly, they don't always want people to tiptoe around them by *not* talking about what happened.

They don't want the horror of it all swept away in an effort to save their feelings. In fact, I read in a beautifully-written book called *Shattered* that most often what non-crime victims don't understand is that crime victims, let's call them survivors, usually *want* to tell again and again what *did* happen – to hear others get scared for them, mad for them, angry on their behalf. It helps to heal, to let the secrecy of it out. A piece of me thinks this is why I write about the crimes of Earl Bradley. So the story can be told.

So this story is *not* swept away or forgotten.

What I Don't Know

What I don't know about child abuse is massive.

What I don't know is the actual feeling of shame described by most sexually abused children.

What I don't know is the humiliation or the horror these children struggle with and may continue to wrestle with for the rest of their lives.

If the abuse happened when they were very young, before they understood what sex was, they struggle with it greatly once they *do* understand.

This is where I feel inadequate writing about the victims because, in truth, I can only imagine.

I cannot understand.

I also know that many of these same victims are now survivors because they have told someone, shared their story and in speaking the words, have released the shame.

I believe that only in this way can they be free.

I believe that when you are abused at a young age, it changes who you *think* you are.

That those abused mourn for what *could* have been. But by talking about it and accepting the past for what it *was*, they give up the hope that the past could have been any different.

The days since December 16th race past me now. Kelly, Maggie and I have raced through the garage door and into the warmth and shelter of our home. I have slammed the door against the harsh winter winds.

Waiting

Thirteen months since the catastrophe of Bradley's arrest and I have grown even more impatient. If that were even feasible.

A seemingly endless lingering sets in.

An interminable delay.

A dull, constant anxiety.

What will we learn about him next? When will the trial actually happen? What about the results on testing him for HIV? Probably only the parents will, one day, learn the answer due to privacy laws. Did the police really bungle the search and seizure of evidence as implied by the defense? What about the impossible possibility of shared pictures of the children on the internet? We, anyone who follows this case, are all counting the days, I think.

The frustrating, nerve-jangling wait. It is as if the future, which I have always measured by my life's length, as most do, now has a distinct endpoint. Whatever lay beyond the hearings, the investigations, the trial, I cannot imagine. It will all be over once *The State versus Earl B. Bradley* trial begins.

The trial. All I can do is count down the fifty or so, long days. The unoccupied afternoons or evenings when worry and curiosity quietly engulf me. The heaviness of the passing minutes, the intense awareness of time, the dizzying sense that the days are too few and then, too long. In the end I am ready for the trial if only because I cannot stand the waiting any longer.

It is now January 2011, just days since the surprise winter storm that slammed into Southern Delaware. The weather changes quickly and suddenly when you live near the ocean. Harsh, cold winds waft up in an instant and race across our corn fields and our sandy beaches. Wildlife seeks shelter. The mounds of smothering snow stop traffic. This storm had choked our beach community similar to the blizzards of last year. Only this one came and went much more quickly.

What is going on, I wonder. The last two winters have seen more snow than the last twenty years on the Delaware coast.

I am at my library writing desk. Overcast skies pour dark light through my skylights. I have pulled on thick, gray woolen socks and a heavy, fuzzy sweater to shield me from the draft. It has been more than a full year thinking, researching and writing about Bradley. Learning more about his lies, about those he hurt – trying to understand the different medical theories about him as well as the legalities of the case against him. And I wait. And I wonder again about the media, the parents, the families. Will most of the parents whose children have been identified be there for the trial? Will many choose not to be? Will there be media from the major cities – New York, Chicago, L.A. or DC? Will I be able to get a seat inside the courtroom? Six weeks until the trial finally begins.

Just as the land has been smothered by the snowfall, so too do I feel smothered. It is a thick, burdensome feeling.

Trial Date and Venue Change

It is still six weeks until the jury is chosen for Bradley's criminal case whose trial will be held in Wilmington, 80 miles North of Lewes. I understand there is no way the prosecution or the defense can find unbiased jurors here in Sussex or Kent counties. But, only recently did I learn from a friend that in Northern Delaware, there are scores of people who have not yet heard of Dr. Earl Bradley. This shocks me since our state is so small; since Wilmington is only eighty miles from Sussex. Eighty: How could they *not* know about this case? They come to our beaches, we read the same newspapers, they shop at our outlets but it's like we're in another state, another land altogether.

And just as the weather constantly shifts, so too does the news. Now I learn that Bradley's trial will *not* be held next month. It will not be held in Wilmington either. Further, it will *not* be a trial by jury, but a bench trial where a single judge will decide Bradley's fate. It will be held in June, over four months from now here in Georgetown, in Southern Delaware, at the Sussex County Courthouse.

The wait begins. Again.

The trial's date change to June comes because of the late ruling from Bradley's evidentiary hearing several months ago. The defense claims that since the ruling was so late, they cannot mount a thorough case for Bradley without more time. So we wait. His defense agrees to a bench trial – if Bradley pleads guilty now, the door than opens for his appeal – the appeal in regard to the alleged *illegal* search and seizure. Because it is a bench trial, both the defense and the prosecution agree to the move back to Sussex County since the need to find non-biased jurors no longer exists.

I could never have guessed that the timing, the place, even the process would change so drastically just a few weeks before the trial was *supposed to* take place. The light in my library takes on a more dreary shadow now - this interminable frustration of waiting returns with a vengeance. I want to scream.

I glance up from my desk and can see through the living room area and beyond the wide windows to the backyard. My view reaches past the deck, past the white fencing and into the distance where the cypress trees separate my property from the corn field. Snow geese litter the pasture, their heads bobbing, searching for frozen, left-over food from autumn. They look like a moving blanket of snow through the trees, appearing to undulate in unison as they search and peck. A sudden noise startles and scatters them – and they take flight. There is no other sound like it – a soaring whoosh like the air underneath a small plane as it leaves land, a loud, fantastic fluttering and squawking – an awe-inspiring sight and sound and for a brief moment, I am feeling a little less burdened.

Auction

News stories about Bradley are coming less frequently these days but a new one appears now in the *Cape Gazette*: There will be an auction of Bradley's personal items which have been held in a storage unit for the last year. The auction is scheduled for Tuesday, January 25. One week away. I am curious. I am also a little excited. What will happen at the auction? I wonder. Who will be there? I imagine these will be unusual characters, perhaps unsavory ones. I imagine this because these may be people who could want to resell Bradley's items for profit. Might these potential buyers also include those affected by Bradley's crimes? And they would then burn what they purchase? I will hear over the next few days that some, perhaps many, are not happy about this auction.

With the news clipping in my lap, I mark the date in red on my desk calendar. I MapQuest directions to the storage place. Items to be auctioned include Buzz Lightyear, arcade rides, games, children's toys, electronics, equipment, artwork and building supplies. Representatives from Secure Self Storage say "the auction is open to the public and anyone interested should come by to see the items." They "did not wish to comment further." *Who would*, I ask myself.

Apparently no one has paid the storage company since Bradley's incarceration. The company is due over $4,000. Again, the blogs go wild: "They should give any money made off Bradley's stuff to charity! They should burn anything in that storage bin that belonged to him!" I'm nervous now, thinking of how many people might be hurt because of this auction – how many reminders or triggers this may inflict on victim family members. Suddenly, this auction seems cruel, like rubbing dirt into a raw wound. This auction represents memories. The bad kind. The kind most want to forget.

Friends of mine who know I follow the case ask if I will go to the auction. When I tell them I will, they are immediately concerned: "Meg, don't get out of your car, the people who go to this thing will be nuts! And *Why* are you going? You don't want any of his junk, do you?" My response is, of course, I won't be buying anything, but I'm curious to see what kind of people turn up for this auction. Will they be like those who attend garage sales every single weekend? Or people who think items of Bradley's might be worth something – people who look for 'collectibles,' regardless if these collectibles are from a madman. Then I think, I am sickened – that one day some of his toys might actually be worth more than they are today. It nauseates me to imagine that anyone would want anything that once belonged to this heinous doctor.

I'm also curious to see what kind of controversy this thing triggers. No doubt reporters will be eager to cover it. Now, I am again starting to feel shame at my own level of excitement. My obsessive curiosity. Is this what others who plan to go to auction are feeling? What is wrong with me I ask, that I have allowed myself to crawl so deeply into this bizarre world? What does this say about *me*, I wonder…am I too one of those nasty thrill seekers, those gawkers who pull over to the side of the road just to watch when there is a car wreck? Or those who stand and watch a burning building for hours as firefighters fight the burn. Hoping to see what? Dead bodies? Or in the case of this auction, angry parents ganging up on the storage company owners because really, all Bradley's things should be destroyed instead of sold, as if they were antique dolls or clocks or some other kind of ridiculous memorabilia. I think for once I will take my friend's advice and *not* get out of my car.

I couldn't have predicted that on January 24th, less than seventeen hours before the auction was due to begin, the owners of Secure Self Storage would cancel the auction when asked to do so by the Attorney General's office. Or that the storage company would sell Bradley's items to the state for the sum total of $1.00.

In writing class one day a friend asked me about the state destroying Bradley's belongings.

"Meg, don't you think it's wasteful that the state would destroy all the toys?" Why wouldn't they donate them to some hospital or charity?"

"How can you ask that?" I snap.

Another woman says, "What do you mean how can she ask that? It's a logical question."

But I don't feel logical or rational about this question.

"Because these are no longer 'just toys.' I say more loudly, more angrily than I want. "What if that Pinocchio doll, the one he used to sodomize one of his victims, fell into the hands of a cancer-stricken child in a hospital? I ask.

"Why does that matter?" my friend said.

Doesn't everybody see that these are no longer *just* toys? That they are symbols of what he did!"

My friends are quiet now.

I am not disappointed that the auction is cancelled. It is right. It is a good thing to do. It is less painful this way. Who knows what kind of people would have shown up at this thing.

Me being one of them.

Perhaps some irate parent would have shown up, pulled out a gun and shot at the toys or worse, a buyer. There is that much residual pain here that I can actually envision this.

Later in the month of January another short article appears on my Google alerts. The Delaware State Police, assisted by Delaware Department of Transportation, have removed items owned by Bradley from the Secure Self Storage Unit. The items were transported to an undisclosed remote facility where they were destroyed, rendered useless and disposed of, never to be resold or utilized again.

Disposed of, rendered useless, destroyed. These words make me think of the items' owner. Such descriptive, final words – the same words I'd use to describe what has become of Earl Bradley.

Priests

A surprise Spring-like day in late February, 2011. I am enjoying lunch on the back deck, reveling in today's rare 70 degree weather. Bright sunshine warms the earth and for two days we will enjoy a respite from winter's gray cold.

While snacking on grilled chicken strips and hummus, I read PEOPLE Magazine, flipping through the colorful, crinkly pages: Pictures of Nichole Kidman's new baby, snapshots of Oscar contenders, best movies, worst dressed, red carpets. Interspersed among celebrity stories are puzzles, human interest stories, search and rescues, grisly murders, an update on the once-trapped Chilean miners asking 'where are they now?' And then I stop: *Did this Priest Hire a Hit Man? Police say a troubled Texas priest did more than molest an underage boy-he also tried to have him murdered.*

I am stunned by the priests' picture; stunned by how much Father Fiala and Earl Bradley look alike. Same age, same stature; the only difference between the two is that Fiala sports a mustache while Bradley wears a full beard. Almost everything else is the same, the shape of their face, their eyeglasses, their hair color and style. Both wear wire rimmed similar-in-shape, coke-bottom lens' eyeglasses. Both squint. Dr. Bradley sports his traditional blue scrubs, Father Fiala, his priest collar. I've gone inside now to my library and place the photos of the men beside each other and can't stop staring. Both men are large, weighing in the 220 pound range. Even their noses are similar in shape with deep-cut laugh lines that curve from nose to mouth.

But it's their fake smiles and empty dark blue eyes that tell the real story.

I am struck as well by other similarities between the criminal case of Father Fiala and the pediatrician, Earl Bradley. *They* are everywhere I think: These natural or man-made mistakes posing as important, well educated, care-takers of the body and soul. A priest and a doctor. It's not only the size of our towns that are similar, but how long Fiala got away with what he was doing to young boys: Almost 22 years. Seven more than Bradley. Is this what most of these cases have in common? The fact that pedophiles get away with it for far too long? Twenty-two years. A quarter of a lifetime, four or five Presidents, time enough for someone to be born and go through college into young adulthood.

In this short story of yet one more madman, I find even the same wording is used: As with Bradley, in the Fiala case, over and over the matter was dropped, the investigation closed. "Father John Fiala, 52 allegedly forced himself on a then 16-year old-boy several times in 2008, twice at gunpoint." His town of Rocksprings, Texas is only slightly larger than Lewes. *Another small community, another pathetic tragedy.*

In Bradley's original hospital staff picture, his smile is weak, disingenuous. As a young man and as a middle-aged man, Bradley did not fit in. He was alone. I can see this in a smile that is not only forced but sad. It is the same type of smile as Father Fiala's. It is the smile of a man desperate to fit in, to be respected. Again, I keep noting the similarities: Both the Priest and Doctor have salt and peppered hair, parted to the right side; both have thick, wrinkled jowls. But their eyes. Both have dead eyes. They are both without connection. They have both chosen powerful careers. Did they think their powerful careers would win them respect? Gain them access to children? Or allow them to connect at all? Where did their lives go wrong?

Part V: Spring 2011

So farewell hope; and with hope farewell fear; Farewell remorse: All good to me is lost; Evil be my good.

-John Milton, Paradise Lost-

Brave

Springtime in Rehoboth and opening day of the Farmers' Market; a fabulous, *lucky* Tuesday May 2nd 2011. Sixty-five degrees and a deep, moist wind from the ocean rustles through my hair. I call it lucky since it is one of those days when I feel my destiny, my good fortune, to live here. I have days like that. Often.

But today, ah today, Osama Bin Laden was killed. He is dead. A small smile escapes my lips as I think back to this morning's news. I cannot stop saluting in my head, those Special Ops Navy Seals who took the world's #1 enemy off this earth and who, with purposeful insult, dressed him in a white sheet, tilted and slid his body into the depths of the ocean. No grave, no grave marker. As if, he never existed. He is *rendered useless*. I watched the news this morning for hours: Grateful Americans celebrate his death with song and signs that read *Ding, Dong Bin Laden is Dead*. American flags billow in front of the White House and in New York City. I can't help but wonder how our community and mostly the families affected by Bradley's crimes, will celebrate *his* conviction or *his* inevitable death some day.

The Farmer's Market is alive with hopeful vendors, fresh lavender from Lavender Fields, fish peddlers, colorful flowers and green plants interspersed with bread that smells of thyme and rosemary. The scent of sugar and herbs is everywhere. A bearded, baseball-capped vocalist on his wooden stool strums a guitar and sings ballads. He is lovely. The world feels so very lovely today.

As I stroll past the white merchant tents, I think of how a generation of children born around 9.11 never knew a world without Bin Laden. Without terror. And I think again about how many of our town's children, born in a similar timeframe, didn't know a world without Earl Bradley. How those from both New York and Southern Delaware were forced to grow up very fast, how their outlook on life would be darker, how their childlike sense of safety might be lost. The children in NYC grew up in color coded terror alerts, massive security restrictions, bomb sniffing dogs.

Bradley's victims would grow up in a twisted, similar way - fighting a different war on a different kind of terror.

Sheriff's Sale

Bradley's business property is in foreclosure and goes to sheriff's sale on May 17. Finally. This eyesore land with its overgrown grass and weeds, the decaying buildings and brick-brak toys heaped in a junk pile behind the rotting fence – everything from his medical practice on Coastal Highway, will be sold. I presume the new owners will demolish the buildings and sheds that stand on this land and they will rebuild.

Except. At this sheriff sale, which is where they will auction off Bradley's business to the highest bidder…there *are* no bidders. Not one single person decides to purchase this prime real estate along Highway 1 within minutes of our pristine beaches.

I think back to the auction that was cancelled a few months ago. Once the state stepped in and spent the dollar to buy all of Bradley's ugly symbols, symbols of his crimes, they had been *rendered useless* and then *destroyed* by the state. *Rendered useless* is another one of the phrases that floats through my brain again and again as I write these pages. Bradley, his property, his belongings, his life…all, *rendered useless*. Who else would be *rendered useless* because of this case?

I think again of Bin Laden's death. And another thought is, just as the sacred grounds of the twin towers are being rebuilt, and will soon open to the public, can't Bradley's property also, be – rebuilt? Is this what closure is about? About tearing down the ugly, terror ridden symbols of the past and making way for a hopeful future?

Publish?

Bright sunlight streams into the front of the book store from Rehoboth Avenue, our main street that leads to the ocean. Today it is packed with spring break students and early off-season tourists. Main Street swells with people laughing, dogs barking, drivers searching for parking spaces.

I walk into Browseabout Books, one of very few independent, old-fashioned book stores still in existence. I *love* this store. Nothing like the large book store chains, the atmosphere is quiet and serious with a warm, welcoming sense to it. It might be the fresh brewed coffee or the owner or manager who greets customers with a smile or even the intoxicating smells of the bath products - lavender, rose and peppermint wafting through the air. Other products perfectly displayed on tables and shelves embrace the sea – the blues and greens of the ocean, white starfish, sandy colored tea towels and plate ware.

Beach-themed sweatshirts, books, magazines, periodicals and greeting cards beckon. But there isn't time to shop. In the back of the store under harsh fluorescent bulbs twenty people have come to learn about publishing their own books – children's books, crime stories, memoirs and fiction. It doesn't matter the genre. Today, while the average age of the group is somewhere around fifty, we're all eager students. The session is starting so I take my seat in one of those metal chairs, shoulder to shoulder with other would-be writers. Paper handouts crinkle, people whisper, grab their coffees and Cokes and settle in for the two-hour workshop.

After just fifteen minutes, my head begins to swim with details about how the printing, pre-press and graphic design industry have changed; about vanity houses, small print firms, the big six, print-on-demand and ways to self-publish. The costs to self-publish are staggering. And then the speaker asks, "After learning what it takes to publish, do you really want to publish your book, and more importantly, why?" I can't get this question out of my head.

I think about it long after the workshop ends.

I *thought* I wanted to publish this book, but now I feel anxious and overwhelmed. Why? I'm worried not only *how* I might publish it but "Is it good enough for publication at all?" And "Who will want to read it?" I learn about bringing my book to market, but which market? I wonder. My angst starts to feel overwhelming for at the core of this insecurity, I have to ask again "Is it good enough? Am *I* a good enough writer?

Ruling

I think back to Judge Carpenter's ruling that the thumb drive videos showing Bradley raping children had been *legally* seized from his office and that this evidence will be permitted at trial. I, like many, had waited for this ruling for eight months. The defense wanted the evidence thrown out; the prosecution didn't. Finally, we have not only a decision – but the right decision.

With the judges' decision in a 43-page ruling, I feel like I can breathe again. I didn't realize until now that I've been in a continued state of limbo. Imagine. Bradley could have gotten off on a technicality. Could that really have happened? I realize that certain legal rules are there to protect the innocent, but they sometimes end up protecting the guilty.

As I sit in the bookstore, I glance around and think how this store represents community. How many people in the *How to Publish a Book* audience have a connection in some way to the case? And what will happen to our community if the hospital, as a result of the suits, closes? Was anyone else in this store thinking about the Bradley case as I was, as I do, every day?

A hand rises in front of me and the woman in row three interrupts the speaker. After some back and forth chatter, another speaker steps up to the mic. The question she asks continues to resonate. Why? And do I want to publish this book? What effect could it have on my community? I think I must. Publish it. Whether I self-publish or find an agent, it doesn't matter. I think that many, especially those in the Beebe Hospital Family may not want this story told. I think perhaps the parents of abused children, do. Either way, somehow, it has become my duty to tell it.

The chronicling or documenting of this case and how it affected my community has become too important to just let it go.

Six Weeks

With every passing day it grows more and more warm. I grow more impatient. It is finally time though. The trial will take place soon. Just a few short weeks from now and I can't quite believe it will actually happen. Will it really? I think of that DelawareOnline blogger asking "Why are they putting the parents through this when they know he's guilty? Is this a political ploy by Biden so he can show off at trial? Shouldn't he be offering a plea so the parents don't have to go relive it?"

My reply to this blogger would have been: Did you ever think that this is what the parents want, that it is <u>their</u> wish to see him get what he deserves, for *their* own closure?"

Part VI: Summer 2011

STILL

She won't talk about him or what he did to her. She is four now.

Still, when she hears his name she covers her ears. She shakes her head back and forth. She cries, her memory, insistent.

Still her parents are laden with guilt.

They want him to suffer. They want him to rot in hell.

They trusted him. They thought they needed him.

Two years later the children that Bradley sexually molested still hurt. Their parents remain in a suspended state of pain.

It may be a lifelong journey for the families to move on. To persist. To heal.

So he doesn't haunt them anymore. So it doesn't define them anymore.

So they are victims, no more.

Two years ago. A respected doctor. Arrested. The rape of over 100 children.

Still they suffer.

The Trial

June 7. In Delaware, it is billed as the "Trial of the Century." But it ends in less than six hours of testimony. Those six hours leave me in a different sort of despair, one I have never experienced before. Ever.

A brutal summertime heat hits early this year, June. It is nearly ninety degrees the morning I rush to get my seat at the trial of Earl Bradley. I arrive forty minutes before it is due to begin, search for a parking space and can't find one that allows me more than two hours of parking. I will have to feed the meter, I think, slamming the car door and moving quickly through the heavy white double doors of the Sussex County Courthouse. Once I make it through security, and after officers seize my Kindle, I wonder, where is everybody?

There are TV cameras, broadcasters and crews in front of the courthouse but I thought the entire building would be teaming with parents, CAC (Child Advocacy Center) representatives, more press. The carpeted hallways are empty except for the line of people who wait near a courtroom on the main level for misdemeanor violations, traffic offenses, drunk and disorderly, etc.

Am I too late? Are there so many people already inside courtroom number one that there are no seats left? I worried about this prospect for days, even stopping by the Cape Gazette office and asking its publisher, whom I'd met, if he'd 'lend' me a press pass. No luck. I hadn't thought there would be, really.

I set out to find my courtroom, asking several official-looking people where it is. A new feeling assaults me, one I haven't felt before. An inkling of shame – like I am one of those vulture paparazzi who'd come to see what the legal system does to a monster. Is that what these officers and clerks think I am...a story-starved journalist...desperate to get the latest on the man who destroyed hundreds of lives?

Eighteen months, over 500 days of sleeping, eating, breathing Bradley.

Perhaps, I *am* one of those people.

The courtroom is much larger, more comfortable than the room of the probable cause hearing ten months earlier. Rows of polished wooden benches with green and beige striped seat cushions this time. It is not dark or strangely cold like the other courtroom. Sunlight streams in through the large curtained windows behind the judges' raised bench. It is comfortable. The antitheses to what today would be.

This courtroom is larger than the last one I'd visited. Still, it is split into two sides. On the right sit approximately seventy parents or relatives and a handful of CAC officials. Twenty minutes to the start of the trial and I take my seat on the left side next to two dozen reporters who are already scribbling away. Bradley's two defense lawyers take their seats on the left side up front. The prosecution which consists of four, enter. Attorney General Beau Biden is the final attorney to take his seat.

I don't understand why, but both legal teams are escorted from the courtroom just before 10am. I learn later that this is when the judge tells both the prosecution and defense how he'll run his courtroom; what his expectations are; how *he'll* control the proceedings.

10:00 a.m. approaches. I feel a queasy mixture of tension in the air.

Every minute past 10:00, it gets worse.

Clenched stomachs, guttural anger. Anguish that at any moment Bradley will enter the room. I try to lighten my own tension by looking around: A video camera on the right side, although I don't know if it is recording anything. Many more chairs to accommodate the prosecution than the defense. Three lone chairs for Bradley, his only public defender and his assistant. The mumbling in hushed, nervous tones of people talking grows louder and louder until an officer of the court asks everyone to speak more softly. It seems that the louder everyone speaks, the more it increases tension levels. Perhaps this is why he asks attendees to tone down their voice.

I realize one of the press representatives has left his seat and it has been a while since returning. Taking his spot, I move to the end of the bench, center aisle for a better view. The teams re-enter and the atmosphere feels even heavier as the bearded, straggly-haired Bradley enters the courtroom from the left chamber door flanked by a guard. Again he is in hand cuffs and shackles. He is even thinner than the last time. There is a collective gasp.

The disgust is palpable.

The silence, supreme.

The glares, ferocious.

Bradley shuffles to his seat and head bowed looks up for an instant.

People look away.

And so it begins.

Testimony

I could never have known how horrific the testimony would get that afternoon. Six hours in total, two of which are so gruesome something in me snaps. For the first time it becomes more than real. It is almost surreal. The betrayal, the children's pain, the parent's pain, the brutal testimony from the computer forensics detective; the disclosure that some girls appeared to lose consciousness, both choking and suffocating when he forced oral sex on them; how they clawed at his legs as they howled in pain and fear.

How he'd used a recurring word - the word 'popsicle.'

How he'd told some parents that the sugar in the popsicle was good for the toddlers after they'd been given injections.

How "He'd be right back" after taking them to the checkerboard building for their *treat*.

How sometimes he'd smear their faces with a cherry popsicle to cover up the blood that seeped from their cut mouths.

A gruesome procession of awful details.

Revulsion wells within me. I feel the blood drain to my feet. Everything seems suddenly fuzzy like wet cotton has been stuck in my ears. I think, smearing ice cream…smearing grief.

Other times, his belly suffocated the children's airways.

Nothing this extreme. Nothing this insane.

I cannot believe the level of violence. I catch a glimpse of Bradley. He is just sitting there staring straight ahead, calm, seemingly disinterested but what I saw in my head, was a wild animal ripping at its prey. For one brief moment I *am* one of those parents. I try to search the parents' eyes and watch the CAC lady jumping from parent to parent as they hug one another, rest their heads on each other's shoulders. Tissues are everywhere. Everything is suddenly happening in slow motion. My chest feels tight.

For the first time, it isn't all in my imagination or something I read or someone I spoke to. I try to stay seated thinking maybe no one notices my shoulders shaking or that I'm desperately trying to stifle the tears. Maybe they don't know I'm about to puke.

But it is when Detective Garrett says, "Just a month before his arrest, Bradley filmed himself with a 6 month old baby using both hands to "clamp" her head while forcing her to perform oral sex," that I run. I feel like I am running for my life, like this crushing grief is taking me and that I too am suffocating.

The words begin to rain down, slamming into me.

They pillage. I am no longer in control.

I shoot out of my seat. There is no thought behind my movement. I run for the crash doors just a few feet away. Through heaving tears, a shudder moves through me, only it is slow. I can't feel my feet or my hands. Only my heart pounds as I run from the testimony for the first time.

There will be a second.

Just steps away from the courtroom doors, the wall bolstering me, I keep wiping away the tears but know there are more to come. The lump in my throat won't go away. I compose myself, slither back in, feeling embarrassed I ran in the first place.

Upon my return Detective Garland is already discussing another child: "And when he was done, he flung her onto the couch, tossing her two feet in the air." By this point, the child was unconscious so when he threw her, it was like he was discarding a rag-doll." The detective went on to describe how Bradley screamed at the little girls, slapping them, trying to revive them once their ears and lips turned blue. Even the detective said he screamed at the computer screen, yelling, "Wake up, dammit, wake up!" This particular child had been drugged with nitrous oxide and attacked in Bradley's home. She was seven-years-old.

My reaction surprises me - I don't just cry. I am as close to hysterical as I've ever come. I run for the second time and this time one of the CAC women follows me. I grab for the large white window ledge just outside the courtroom.

I am afraid now. That I'll faint or that I'll vomit. I keep telling myself to calm down. The CAC woman who followed me out of the courtroom is kind, handing me water, letting me talk, offering me tissues. I talk about my guilt. My own guilt.

"I have no right to cry. That should be for the parents," I say.

She assures me that this feeling I'm afraid of, or guilty about... is compassion. That it is alright to feel it. I shouldn't feel guilty. Everyone in this room is overwhelmed with different types of grief. Different kinds of outrage.

I sniffle, swallow a sip of water and realize my eyes are swelling. Taking two deep breaths I attempt to pull back the tears and pull myself together. I re-enter the room, shoulders scrunched together, trying to hide the fact that I'd tried to escape these painstaking details. Again.

For the millionth time, I wonder what the hell am I doing – why am I even here?

I am not alone. Half the room whimpers; a profusion of tears. Later Detective Garland's voice cracks as would one of the prosecutor's voices when she reads each one of the now-condensed charges against Bradley. It takes her a half hour to read through 24 charges. I try to imagine if the counts of rape and abuse had held at 500.

No one from the press side cries which makes me feel more guilty since I sit on their side trying to write, trying to keep up, scribbling through the tears. One father storms out, blasting the door with his palm. It sounds like a gunshot so that those in the courtroom jump. I dare not turn around to look.

Half way through the testimony, the air is so tension-filled it feels like the thick beach fog I wrote about so often before.

Detective Scott Garland says, "The violence was beyond anything I expected or had ever experienced."

There are sentences, or partial sentences that penetrate through the nausea like "He used nitrous oxide. Child is asleep. Child is unresponsive. He masturbates on the inner folds on the vagina....Child is out cold." I find I am breathing hard again, but they are shallow breaths, as if the air I breathe has disappeared. And I want to run again but force myself to stay seated. Heartsick over these gruesome details, I wonder how these parents are standing the onslaught. How brave they are as I scrunch my eyes shut against horrid words that tumble through the courtroom.

Driving Home

I barely make the drive home safely. My eyes stay wet most of the way home. After taking care of the dogs, I collapse and fall asleep. It is only 5:00, late in the afternoon. I wake to a blaze of white sun, the burning, searing kind. It is steamy at the end of the day, August-like and rare for this time of year. There is a sour pain in my gut. Waking, I think there are still more questions. It appears now I may never get the answers I've searched for. I still don't know how or why he hurt the children. And these questions would never be asked now, nor would they be answered.

The next day, another hot day and I am feeling bereft, like someone died. I force myself to scan my notes from the trial. I started out writing so carefully, my words small and concise so I could later read my own writing. Fifteen pages on a little lined steno pad – pages and pages that by the end were sloppy and crinkly from dripping tears. The words on the pages grow larger and larger at the point where Detective Garland gave his testimony. Those same words that had me running from the room. My handwriting toward the end of the trial is shaky and so large only ten words fit on a page.

Aftermath

Where shall I begin? I try to write the words of the 'Trial of the Century.' Five hundred and forty days of writing about him, in flashbacks, flash-forwards, listing techniques, setting, physical descriptions, internal/external thoughts, research and a myriad of evidence that generates more and more questions. Just so I can get something down on paper

I begin at the testimony. But it ended as quickly as it began. A bench trial over in six gut-wrenching hours. For me, on that hazy Tuesday afternoon in June, my eighteen month quest to understand Bradley came to an end. I feel, though, more hopeless than I felt before. Despair, shards of it, seem to overtake me. It will be months before I am able to face how the trial had broken me and begin to write about it.

Justice

June 23rd. There is more press here this time around. From Philadelphia, New York, Baltimore. The trucks with their network call letters and satellite polls wrapped in heavy wired rings are as high as the courthouse tower and surround the Sussex County Courthouse. There seem to be more lawyers in the audience this time. Why? For the civil suits? For the man that ultimately bought Bradley's business property, which has been in foreclosure for two months now? I think this only because of the way they are dressed: Expensive suits and watches and flashy, colorful ties. There are more parents here this time. I know. I counted them at trial and now today. Lately, when I think about or am writing about the families, I no longer refer to them as victims but as survivors.

What is more confusing today is that there are fourteen guards in the courtroom.

Delaware Department of Corrections officers.

Once again hazy sunlight filters through the large windows behind the imposing judge's bench and colorful cushions lay on the dark stained wooden seats. This time, what is different is the air - the emotional atmosphere in this room today. A feeling of relief, a brighter, more optimistic truth,

that it will be over soon,

that he *will* be found guilty.

There is no question of this.

At three-twenty, the defense and prosecution re-enter the courtroom through a heavy honey-toned wood door. They take their seats when suddenly men and women in the blue DOC uniforms take strategic positions throughout the courtroom. I am feeling pinned in, claustrophobic, there are so many of them. Three down the center aisle, two on each side of the courtroom – <u>six</u> of them proceed Bradley's entrance. They form a semi-circle around where he seats himself. He faces the judge; the guards face us. Bradley looks up briefly but his eyes quickly divert to the ground. He appears as a schoolboy might. One who has been scolded.

Every one of the officers take a 'fight stance' legs spread, arms folded. Three-twenty-two, the chime goes off and the "All Stand" is declared as Judge Carpenter takes his seat behind the large wooden bench.

While the raised bench area is intimidating, Judge Carpenter is the opposite. He is of a shorter stature, stocky and appears non-imposing with his tousled hair – someone who looks like your every-day soccer Dad with a kindly demeanor about him. I could like this man, I think. I know I highly respect him and the way he's handled this case. My eyes dart around the room from one officer to the next. There was only one guard at trial two weeks ago, the one who'd escorted Bradley into the courtroom. I don't understand why there are fourteen this time. Neither do the reporters or media reps I sit next to.

Later I find out that these guards helped escort each one of the parents out the back door of the courtroom, where the press are not allowed. Was it out of respect to the parents? Or to protect them from gossip-hungry press? Was it simply a nod to the seriousness of Bradley's crimes? More likely, there may have been another, maybe more significant, threat on Bradley's life since the trial.

I don't know the answer to this question – I do know that Bradley's battle has just begun as his defense begins to fight for him all over again after today. They will focus on filing their appeal within the next thirty days. Perhaps this is why there is no victory felt in the courtroom today. We all know it isn't really, completely, over.

Still, today, the once-respected pediatrician Earl B. Bradley was found guilty on all counts of first and second degree rape and the sexual exploitation of a child. The word, even though I knew it would come, ricochets through me like a pin-ball firing off a game's side-rails.

Guilty.

On this hot, sticky day, a Thursday in late June, a type of justice, deceptive as it may be, comes to eighty-six young children and their parents who had been victimized and who had survived a sick predator. Once charged with molesting 127 children, this number had been reduced at trial two weeks earlier because 19 children remained unidentified – and probably never would be…identified. Other parents of those he raped could not bring themselves to be involved in the case for very valid reasons – most having to do with their personal feelings about their child's future well-being. I came to learn that the average age of those molested was three years old – some as young as three *months* old. Again, an unimaginable statistic. The number of counts against him had also been condensed to 24 versus the 527, which either way, carries the life-in-prison penalty. Since his sentence was virtually the same for 24 or 527 counts, my understanding for the condensing of the charges was a matter of time constraints. It took over forty minutes just to read 24 counts – imagine if a court clerk had to read 527.

Verdict

Sentencing is slated for August 26, two months from now. Head down, scribbling as fast as the judge speaks, I smile. It is a sad but knowing smile.

The word anti-climactic is defined as *an ordinary/ unsatisfying event that follows an exciting or dramatic series of events of increasing anticipation.* Today's hearing is the epitome of this word. Eighteen months since his arrest and it comes down to a twenty-five minute ruling by one judge, no jury. A tension-filled half hour after a late start as Judge Carpenter slowly and deliberately defines, in legal terms such depraved words as rape, assault, child abuse.

Other terms begin to blur: Reviewed all the evidence...state has met its burden to prove... sustained physical injury...defendant stood in trust, acted knowingly, recklessly....and at the end of each bundle of charges, "The state finds the defendant guilty on all counts."

When he is finished, no one claps, no one shouts, no one jumps out of their seat. I, on the other hand feel compelled to do...something. What? Shout? Jump up and down? But I don't. I can't shake the feeling, though: Isn't there supposed to be some joy, some feeling of divine justice in this room today?

But there is no victory lap.

No words of condemnation for Bradley. This, I presume, will come two months from now at sentencing. What there is, as it was two weeks ago, is the never-ending stream of tears, hands clasped around shoulders, more tissues as each charge is painstakingly read. *Guilty. Guilty. Guilty.*

Although I want to jump out of my seat, a wall of sadness pushes against me – it feels like someone's hand pressing flat against my chest forcing me to stay seated. My emotions are so jumbled at this point, I can't decipher them anymore. And if *I* feel this way, what must the parents feel?

Razing

Now that the trial and decision have come and passed, I await the court date of his sentencing. Early in the month of August, I read another article in the *Gazette*, that someone had purchased the land where Bradley's medical buildings are located.

It is the August 9th edition of the Gazette where I learn that a local real estate developer, Bruce Geyer, has purchased his property and wants to make clear his intention to raze the buildings as soon as possible. In a statement to the paper he says, "It bothers me badly." He also states, '"He will not step foot on his new property until the buildings are gone."

With temperatures approaching 100 degrees this afternoon, I head off to one of my coffee places for a frosty iced coffee. Dodging summer traffic, I think back to how long people have been talking about tearing down his medical practice. Two months? Twelve? There is some surprise that no one took it into their own hands to burn it to the ground earlier.

A week later I learn that Harry Caswell, an 'everybody knows him' kind of guy, an air conditioning contractor in Long Neck, has volunteered to take down the buildings where Bradley committed his crimes.

I know I will be there on that day.

I wonder: What business will be viable here on this property?

I wonder: Can anyone ever rid it of the horrific crimes that happened here? Will the ghosts of those crimes linger for generations?

At least the buildings will no longer have to be viewed by drivers racing down Route 1 in Lewes. Out of sight, out of mind? I think not - at least not for many years to come.

The electric doors of the café swing open and oven hot heat blasts my face when I step outside; even my hair feels hot. I quickly take a sip of the icy coffee from the cup that is already sweating. And as I drive home, the wind of the air conditioning in my face, one of those writing insecurities resurfaces like a snake slithers from its hole.

It is the insecurity about my struggle to tell this story adequately enough. One of the most common of my self-doubts is that aside from people not wanting to read this story, the truth is that some stories just don't have happy endings. As I fall asleep that night to the sound of soft rain, I wonder how good of a writer I'd need to be to make a happy ending to a story about abused children. Is it even possible? I think not for this story.

Sometimes

August 2011 is a month of extremes in Sussex County Delaware. Residents feel the tremors of an earthquake measuring 5.9 on the Richter scale, although it is some 200 miles from the epicenter in central Virginia. During this week, Hurricane Irene and tornadoes strike our coastal towns. And on this same weekend, the one just before Labor Day, our beach area loses over 50 million in tourism dollars over the three days of evacuations and storms.

Sometimes I still look back and ask *why* am I doing this? New answers come along as the days melt and fade and fold...away.

Sometimes I think this story may be more about lost faith than about the struggle to understand him. Is this, really, about *my* lost faith and my attempt to reclaim it?

Sometimes it feels like we are cursed. Like some evil spell has been cast upon our salty shores.

On Friday, August 26th the day before Hurricane Irene slams into the East Coast, I evacuate alongside thousands of others. With winds predicted to be over 100 miles per hour, I find myself driving...fast; westward along Route 16 through the tiny brick-fronted, train-tracked towns of Ellendale and Greenwood and beyond into Maryland toward the windy Bay Bridge. At exactly 9:55 AM it strikes me, like someone just clicked on a light: I was supposed to be at the courthouse for Bradley's sentencing. I pull over in Denton, Maryland knowing I will soon be cruising out of the local radio station's listening range, and sit there waiting for the verdict. The light coming through the car windows is darker now with unnaturally green-black clouds. The air smells damp and heavy; quiet. And as the air becomes heavier, so too does the traffic as people race away from the coast.

My first evacuation; my first potentially dangerous hurricane. It's interesting how your thought process gets mangled when you're faced with a life-threatening situation. Friends called from all over the country telling me to leave town. The weather channel said leave; the state's governor said mandatory evacuation. This includes four phone messages from the state's emergency management system.

So I leave. Dogs, food, water, meds and clothes were all I could think of that Friday morning. I toss everything into the hatch-back of my golden Murano, dogs in the middle, food in front and off to Alexandria, Virginia I run. On my way west, I think, what about my photos? What about my business? What about the story I'd been writing...about him. I forgot almost everything else important in my life except the absolute basics. I suppose this is what is meant by panic.

Sentencing

Meanwhile, Bradley is again capturing the media spotlight despite Hurricane Irene. And I am going to miss the finale. It is now 10:30. A bright yellow Shell sign looms overhead. I sit in my car and wait until 10:35 when Bradley is sentenced to fourteen life sentences for first degree rape and 164 years in prison for second-degree assault and the sexual exploitation of a child.

The thing I'm most aware of is my own response to this news. I don't shout out. I don't catch my breath or burst into tears. I feel utterly and pervasively blank. And then I am consumed with trying to understand what I'm supposed to do with this news. My brain is standing still, like a button got stuck. I almost laugh out loud, the news, the sentencing, the place where I'm sitting listening, is so absurd. But I find a smile spreads slowly across my lips and I think this punishment is *enough*. Short of a death sentence, *it is enough*.

Intermittent drops of rain splash on my windshield. I listen as the case that dragged on for close to two years ends. And just as the hurricane will hit not with an explosion but a whimper, so too will Bradley's case limp along to its close.

I swallow hard and stare down at the seat beside me, a pink-soled Asics sneaker, a bag of pretzels, a small red and white cooler filled with apples, grapes and diet Coke. The dogs are puffing in the back seat. Maggie, as always must touch me – she has her nose nuzzled into my shoulder. Just before pulling away, the radio announcer relates Judge Carpenter's final words to Bradley:

"You have abused your position. You have violated the morals of your community. You will never be a doctor again and never again be in a position to violate a child."

I open the window wide and pull out onto Route 404.

It is enough....short of him dying.

Later I will read that Paula Ryan, the Sussex County Prosecutor says, "no jail time is sufficient to address the damage Bradley has done. He committed unspeakable acts, repeatedly attacking toddlers and children and videotaping it for his own perverse pleasure."

"Bradley groomed parents to trust him to get access to their children; a sophisticated and dangerous pedophile who cunningly, deceitfully manipulated parents. The damage is devastating and far-reaching. Parents should not blame themselves for allowing Bradley's crimes to happen. Only Earl Bradley is to blame."

I cannot imagine what prosecuting this case has meant to Ryan. She was the one who, when we were in court, read all the charges against Bradley aloud. She is the one whose voice cracked while reading those charges. I cannot imagine her level of hatred toward this man – I can only imagine her relief now that it is over.

I wish I could have been there just to watch Bradley's expression. Even if there was none, I would have enjoyed imagining what he might have felt. Inside. Being there would have been worth enduring a hurricane.

Part VII: Fall 2011

*The first evil choice is linked to the second;
And each one to the one that follows,
both by the tendency of our evil nature and by the
power of habit, which holds us as by a destiny.*
Tryon Edwards

Forever

I wake this morning to a crisp, brightly lit kind of day. Our first after this summer's relentless heat. It is mid-September when I receive an early morning Google alert on Dr. Bradley. It must be big news to come this early, I think. The sunlight hours have begun to displace the shadows in my backyard, warming the early fall mums and hydrangea.

Lately, I feel as though I'm coming close to putting an end to the Bradley story. And then this alert lands on my desk: *Bradley Buildings to be Razed on October 10*. Immediately I jot the date on my calendar. A thread of warmth snuggles through me. I am thrilled to read that the demolition will finally take place. That our State Justice Department has come through to do as promised – to not only support, but to fully manage the demolition of the Bradley buildings.

Sometimes I feel I will be writing the ending to this story for months, for years, forever. It feels never-ending – new notions about it continuously invade my thoughts. Before falling asleep last night it occurred to me that this story, like so many, would not be about sin and redemption for I have learned there are some things even God cannot forgive.

Nor can I.

It would be a story about sin and about evil without any redemption whatsoever.

But this story would also be about a middle-aged woman who after finding the small town existence she'd searched for throughout her adult life, instead finds a glimmer of hell. Although she loves this place, her faith and belief system get damaged as late in life as age sixty. How can that be? Don't we know, certainly, who we are by this time in our lives? But this story has shaken her. Somehow it has injured her or at least scraped a part of her. It will take time to heal and in doing so, perhaps one of the most important lessons she'll learn is this:

It's not the severity of an event that can alter who we are. It's the way we interpret it, how we choose to respond to it.

And so I write about it. I research it. I work hard to better understand how and why he could have done what he did. I take action which in turn teaches me things that are not always good or noble or pleasant to learn.

And then too, with knowledge comes strength. I think this is at the core of what I have learned and what has helped me keep this little piece of hell in my computer and not in my head, nor in my life. But I'm still not sure about this. That is, one day, will all the awful things I have dwelled on all these months come back to haunt me? Could this piece of hell have damaged me in some way that I am not yet aware of?

It is mid-day already as I write this and the light in my office has changed from bright to dim as clouds darken the slits of my skylights. I pause, lift my fingers from the keyboard and reach for this morning's article about razing the buildings of Bradley's medical practice - something the townspeople have wanted for many months.

"The office buildings along Delaware Route 1 in Lewes that have held many painful memories are slated to be demolished on October 10...on that same day state authorities will remove Bradley's personal property from....Everything is going to be destroyed, 100 percent." These are the words of Harry Caswell, the contractor who organized the volunteer demolition effort.

Caswell, who has been flooded with offers of help, wants to keep the demolition in the hands of professionals, the article says. Glancing down at my hands as they type, I imagine people in their baseball caps and work jeans swinging sledgehammers, wielding giant bats, swinging them with fury, as if it were Bradley himself they are aiming for. I envision their ruthless, brutal, frenzied rage as Bradley's old place of business is *rendered useless*.

Fear

I worry the end of *my* story, the end of *his* story, is approaching. I am fearful too that there will be questions about the book I am writing.

That there may even be some hell to pay.

It's like that when you talk about secrets in a small town.

Another fear is not that readers aren't going to care about this book, but that there are some stories people just don't want to hear.

Or perhaps they will not want to read the ugliness that dwells within its pages.

Mostly my fear is that this book will be viewed as nothing more than a pile of paper or a bunch of jumbled scenes.

What if there is nothing that points to the fact that my heart circulates through these words?

Or that my angst binds these pages together?

I am frustrated too that I don't have more answers than when I started almost two years ago.

Frustrated that I have penned so many words to paper that are less than perfect. And yet I cannot stop, not until they have been strained into a single strand, one extraordinary story.

What drives me to keep going? I think about how many have tried to deter me from doing this. But I am not easily swayed.

Somehow, it has become my job.

A job to write about what others don't want to and to write something that will matter after the book is put back on a shelf somewhere.

As the day wakens, a crack of light has made its way through pulled blinds in my bedroom. It is a day that promises to be a hot sticky one in Delaware although it is early fall and the tourists begin their departure. I cannot believe it is my second fall writing about the Bradley case.

Twenty-two months since the arrest.

Solitude

Solitude is a darker condition than I'd thought ten years ago before starting my own business where I work alone. But the matter of being alone is vastly different than being lonely. Yes, I have been alone for eighteen years since my divorce. And it's been almost a decade since I've had a real love relationship, and four years since a man showed me any interest at all. I'm not a recluse, but sometimes I feel like I hide from people. And sometimes I hide from loving someone. And I wonder what role writing this book has played in my *not* getting out there to search for this relationship. What man would listen to my struggles to write about a pedophile?

This past spring, I told an old boyfriend, whom I still care about some thirty years later, that I was writing this book about the Bradley case. It was toward the end of a reunion, a lovely memory-filled evening, and he walked me to my car. It was midnight and we were still reminiscing when, instead of kissing him goodnight, I began to blather on about the Bradley case and how my writing about it had, somehow, turned into a book. Months later, I still ask myself, "What was I thinking?" How could I have ended a day filled with laughter and sweet memories with the details of a child molestation case?"

Yes, I am alone but not lonely. Not usually. In truth, this story is isolating. But, is writing this story just one more excuse *not* to find that intimate relationship I'm supposed to?

I throw open the blinds to let in the full throttle of today's hazy sunshine and in doing so I struggle to toss my fears aside: *So what* if this book is isolating. And by using this word I mean there's no one to talk to about *my* feelings of sadness as I write; the only refuge for my addiction, is to get those feelings down on paper.

Or to stop.

But I can't. This story, as sad as it is, is an important one to tell.

Finished

It's almost November, another anniversary of my move to the beach. A place where the road is wide open and seems to stretch on for years and years with limitless, infinite, unspoiled possibility.

Have I done that? Taken *real* advantage of small town living – of all the possibilities Rehoboth and Lewes had to offer?

Yes, comes my answer. I 'walk the boards' downtown whenever possible. I run the dogs seaside and shop the outlets and the small shops of Rehoboth and Lewes incessantly. I am involved in local events like Jazz Fest and Film Fest and volunteer for the Autism Ball and work our Writers' Conference to help raise funds.

But most often I sit on the long, wide, empty beach thinking. Dreaming. Reading. Writing. I have met so many new and inspiring people. Artsy, creative, alive and sometimes wild people who opened new doors, who opened my eyes to follow my passion.

To write. And so be it that I wound up filling my pages about a damaged, impaired and now *rendered useless*, doctor.

For a while, everything in my world here at the beach had become a little less magical as I wrote. But now, with the demolition of Bradley's medical practice, possibility flourished again.

Columbus Day Weekend

October 10, Columbus Day weekend 2011 and the heat and humidity returns. I'd heard on the news last night that the ocean's warmer-than-usual temperatures are partly to blame for making the weather here more humid; hotter than it was farther inland. How odd, I think as I near the demolition site, that you can feel the moist heat coming off the ocean this far into fall. Somehow this gives more meaning to what I am about to witness.

But certainly this isn't all I'm thinking of on my drive to what would be the end of Baybee's Pediatrics. Today volunteers in the construction business would eliminate Bradley's place of business.

Demolition

For me, today means something a little different – and part of me is ashamed to admit it – but this will truly put an end to my insatiable obsession. I will no longer be fascinated with each tidbit of Bradley news that drifts to earth via media satellites; I will no longer hang on every word Beau Biden says and I will get fewer and fewer, until I get none – Google alerts on Bradley. How will having written these pages and then its coming to an end, change me? Will the distance of time help cure this addiction?

As I pull into the Lazy Susan Restaurant whose new electronic marquee sign reads "Bradley Demo parking" I wonder, how do you process utter sadness and joy at the very same moment? Sadness that it is coming to an end for me as a writer, sadness that it all ever happened in the first place? Joy that no concrete reminders of him will exist after today.

The demolition, my writing...will all be over in a matter of hours.

Render Useless

The orange Hyundai excavator bucket rips into the building with the sound of crunching metal, wood, door hinges and breaking glass. Debris, millions of minute particles, float into the air. They sparkle in the sunshine and snake into my nostrils and through my clamped lips. I want to spit but don't dare. Pieces of shingles, a red brick fireplace, plastic siding, piping and insulation fall and just as quickly, are crane-scooped and emptied into a total of thirty three dumpsters. The dumpsters are then quickly loaded onto haul trucks, and escorted by police to their final resting ground. No one will ever see or touch any part that was once Baybees Pediatrics. Orange cone barricades, orange fencing, yellow fluorescent construction vests, TV cameras and cops – the evil will soon be gone.

For most of the day, I sit there in one of those collapsible metal chairs, under the white 400 square foot tent typing away on my laptop. A few wonder why and ask me what I am doing – am I a reporter? I respond with a tight smile, a curt nod and reply that I am writing a book on the case.

Still, I am fearful of how people will react to the fact I am working on this story. One woman said "Good. Good for you. I'm glad someone's doing it." Along the way I was not always shown this kind of support.

Some parents are here in a search of closure. They, along with police, prosecutors, volunteers, press and other residents want to see with their own eyes that the nightmare will soon be gone. It started at 7am this morning and all day, every few minutes, another driver passes by honking a happy horn. Another resident gives the thumbs up and flashes a big smile. It is a day of sadness. A day of celebration.

What I don't expect is the joyful symphony of three gigantic cranes and two 10x30 dumpster bins doing such a graceful dance, without crashing into one another with only about five feet between each piece of equipment. I don't expect the utter joy, the glee with which it is accomplished.

Most of that morning holds a more silent, solemn atmosphere. Many just stand there. Glaring. Musing. Crying. Some in disbelief that it is actually happening. Once the main building is torn open I can see the "Wizard of Oz" themed wall with a painted yellow brick road and curtains from the "Little Mermaid" movie featuring Ariel. Hadn't he named one of his children Ariel? And then, the theater stage in the building where Bradley committed and made video recordings of his brutal assaults. Chills run through me even though it is eighty degrees. The giant VW Bug with *Baybees Pediatrics* printed on its side is carved and smashed into unrecognizable pieces. Mike Mocci, one of the volunteer demo experts lifts the car high into the air and then smashes it again and again. When he drives over it, he is heard to say "It's just the right thing to do. I am thinking after all this time how good this feels." I can see the twinkle in his eye - A vengeful smile on his face.

Attorney General Beau Biden, lead prosecutor Paula Ryan, prosecutor David Hume and state police lead detective Scott Garland stand by and watch all day long. Sometimes they clap. Sometimes one of them gives the thumbs up and I watch the detective and Biden shake hands with volunteers or give them the good ol' boy slap on the back as if to say "Good job. Thank you." I feel a kind of community pride in my gut. Something I'd never experienced before.

Sometimes there are hugs.

Sometimes there are tears.

By 1:00 pm the air has changed to one of jubilation. Smiles. Relief. It lingers in the air just as the glittering debris particles had only a few hours earlier. The symphony of destruction is almost over. A sort of Swan song for Bradley's life. Everything in sight physically and symbolically – crumbled, destroyed, devastated.

It's been a few weeks now but every day I drive by where the place used to be, I still have visceral reactions to the absence of it all. Like a phantom limb, you sense it even after it's gone. Only dirt remains. Not a single bush or shrub but a single red letter sign stands with the words "commercial property for lease."

I glance to my right driving south on route 1 and see the ghost of checkerboards where that building used to be. I see in my mind's eye a striped mini-merry-go-round and that bronze statue of kids playing ring-around-the-rosie.

It is finished.

Paradise

In Lewes, Delaware, where Bradley practiced pediatric pedophilia, his story was more far-reaching than {just} rape and child exploitation. Some chalk up his crimes to a string of bad luck – that he ever found our small town in the first place, let alone moved here. Others think it might have been something more sinister. That there might have been other dark forces at play; influences from Satan or some kind of hidden conspiracy. But is our town really that unique to these kinds of small-town shadows, I wonder?

Most don't believe so. What Earl Bradley did is not unique to Southern Delaware. In fact, when the *CBS Evening News* did a report on the town of Lewes and Bradley's case, they disclosed that twenty other pediatricians in several different states had been arrested and convicted for similar crimes to Bradley's over the past decade. The big difference with Bradley is that he made over eighty videos of himself violating his victims.

I learned according to Harvard pediatric professor, Dr. Eli Newburger that a pattern has emerged in pediatrics that is similar to pedophile priests in the Catholic Church: Often these priests are not punished but quietly transferred to other parishes, their behaviors hidden. So too once a medical agency ignores the first complaint against a doctor, they tend to worry more about liability than protecting the victims.

Carry On

No, our town is not so unique. Lewes is similar to other small towns all over the country. It truly can happen anywhere – although I still have trouble believing it happened right down the street from where I live. But there are no dark or sinister spirits at work here nor did we corner the market on pedophiles, misfits and oddballs. The laws have been tightened. There are better reporting mechanisms in place. There is the newly formed and highly successful state's Predator Task Force at work here in Delaware. There is better training given to parents, caregivers, family members and medical personnel alike to spot potential pedophiles living in their midst.

It is the end of October 2011 now. It is warm and humid instead of the usual crisp, cleansing flavor of autumn. Still I struggle to write the ending to Earl Bradley's story – and to mine. I feel tangled in my feelings about what I have written and what I feel inside. I will, though, put an end to my obsession with him today. It is time.

As I approach the final few pages I know I have crossed some imaginary kind of small town line. I have written of what is not spoken of. But as the ache I have felt for so long begins to fade, I know I have started the quest to become whole again.

I know that this is still a place where people come when they want to live in a postcard type setting. It is the kind of place that is easy to visit and difficult to leave. Friends and family pull us back; as does the nature and the beauty of this seaside community. These seaside towns, towns like

Rehoboth and Lewes, represent some of the best that life has to offer.

I know that one day soon I will again stroll through the brick and cobble-stoned streets of Lewes with Maggie and Kelly by my side. I will smile and say "Good Morning," as I pass by neighbors, something I never did in Fairfax, Virginia. Smile at strangers that is. I will pick up coffee at the Lewes Bake Shop. I will wander through the new book store in town, Biblion, the one that sells gently-used books and those written by local authors. Afterward, with King's Ice Cream just steps away I will sit at one of the old-fashioned Formica-topped tables softly lit by wall-hung Victorian-styled sconces. Kings. With its hand-carved framed mirrors, its thin-planked white-washed ceilings and original pine flooring, I am whisked back in time forty years ago to when the ice cream parlor was first born. There, after relishing a cup of coconut fudge ice cream, I will sit and write.

Everything will be as it once was.

I will no longer hear the hushed whispers of disgust about the Bradley case in every store or coffee shop as I once did. Many of the signs of him are gone.

Except in the pages I have written.

I would say to long-time locals or to recent arrivals to the beach that the story of what happened here may seem like an implausibly bad dream. In a place often confused with paradise, it's easy to forget as you would a dream that melts from memory. Years from now, might the story of what Bradley did become some sad tale or worse yet, folk lore?

Perhaps, local legend. But isn't this just one more reason why I chose to chronicle the story:

To preserve the truth.

Because it *did* happen.

It was real.

Hidden Truths

I *do* still love living in Rehoboth right next door to the lovely town of Lewes.

At times, to have lived through this horror in this charming, picturesque town, felt so paradoxical. So ironic.

It made me feel like the possessed observer of misery or the constant chronicler of distress. Trying not to intrude. Trying to just stay quiet, like a counselor might and simply listen to parents' stories.

And yes, I *had* raced toward the beaches of Lewes and Rehoboth years ago with the idea of transforming my life. Little did I know how much those dreams would change once I got here.

How I'd find some hidden truths in my own life.

How I'd lose a large piece of the naïve trust that had been a driving force in my life for far too long.

How writing this would, bring into my life a kind of numbing sadness. For a time. And…it would bring into my life

my own realization of profound loss.

I believe I experienced the victim families' loss in smaller, more accessible ways. A rationing of their loss, bestowed in pieces and bits between research and human grief that sometimes tore me apart. I absorbed their grief, slowly, and in doing so I might have touched a larger loss inside myself. It wasn't a softening I felt. It certainly wasn't forgiveness. It was something else; a letting go of my own failures, or regrets, or losses.

It would be the thousands of deafening, swirling snow geese who glide gracefully through the skies, who remind me of our places of brokenness.

The wild geese soar above our cornfields – they descend upon the parched, dried stalks and stubble of the field behind my home each winter and remind me of my places of sorrow.

Just as the birds stitch up the sky, what we do is pass through here.

Choosing the best path we can, fighting the battle between our worst impulses and our better selves,

the best way we can.

The End

Made in the USA
Middletown, DE
10 July 2023